Osborn Hamiline Oldroyd

Lincoln's Campaign

The Political Revolution of 1860

Osborn Hamiline Oldroyd

Lincoln's Campaign
The Political Revolution of 1860

ISBN/EAN: 9783337812669

Printed in Europe, USA, Canada, Australia, Japan

Cover: Foto ©ninafisch / pixelio.de

More available books at **www.hansebooks.com**

LINCOLN'S CAMPAIGN

OR

The Political Revolution of 1860

BY

OSBORN H. OLDROYD

Author of "A SOLDIER'S STORY OF THE SIEGE OF VICKSBURG," Etc.

PROFUSELY ILLUSTRATED

"Fun and Furore of the Canvass;
Song and Sentiment of the Party."

With Fourteen Portraits and Biographies of Presidential Possibilities
for 1896

CHICAGO
LAIRD & LEE, PUBLISHERS

CONTENTS.

	Historical Introduction	1
I.	Early Movements in Illinois for Lincoln	5
II.	The National Democratic Convention and the Secession from its Ranks	10
III.	The Constitutional-Union Convention	23
IV.	The National Republican Convention	26
V.	Lincoln Apprized of His Nomination	75
VI.	Ratification of the Nomination at Lincoln's Home and the Visit of the Committee from the Convention	78
VII.	Endorsing the Nomination of Lincoln and Hamlin	86
VIII.	Letters of Acceptance	94
IX.	More Ratifications and Indorsements	97
X.	Origin and Splendid Work of the Wide-Awakes of 1860	104
XI.	The Lincoln Demonstration at Springfield, August 8, 1860	110
XII.	The Adventures of a Lincoln Rail	113
XIII.	Leonard W. Volk's Bust of Lincoln from life—Casts of Face and Hands	114
XIV.	Two Great Speeches from Seward and Schenck	120
XV.	A Pen-Sketch of Abraham Lincoln	125
XVI.	The Fusion Candidates	129
XVII.	"Old Abe" Receiving the News of His Election	133
XVIII.	Charles Sumner's Great Speech on Lincoln's Election	146
XIX.	Campaign Songs	150
XX.	Campaign Fun and Caricatures	183

Campaign of 1896.

Illustrated Biographies of Leading Presidential Possibilities - 207

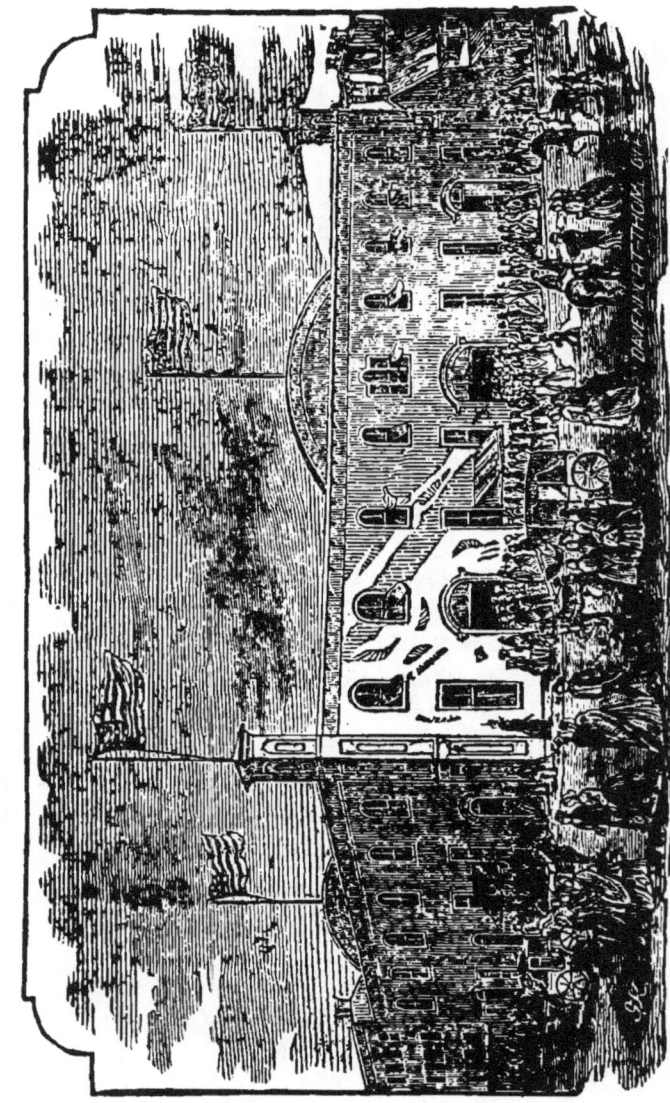

THE CHICAGO WIGWAM,
Where the Republican Convention of 1860 was held.

HISTORICAL INTRODUCTION.

The political campaign of 1860 will go down in history as one of intense excitement. It was composed of four tumultuous and exciting Conventions, each nominating candidates for President and Vice President of the United States. The Republican candidates were Lincoln and Hamlin. The Democratic party was flying with two wings, Douglas and Johnson representing the North, Breckinridge and Lane the South; finally Bell and Everett stood for the "Constitutional Union Party."

It has been our aim to give a correct and impartial history of these Conventions, together with their platforms. The material has been gathered from the "New York Herald," "Springfield (Illinois) Journal" and from other authentic sources of information, and it is confidently claimed that the volume will be useful as a book of reference and of historical worth.

We have reproduced many of the badges, medals, songs and other emblems that formed so prominent a part in the great campaign of 1860, the second in date, but the first in importance in the history of the Republican party, and hope they will be interesting as an illustration of the make-up of a Presidential Canvass.

The Republican Convention of 1896 will be similar to that of 1860, in respect to the prominent men who will be candidates. In 1860 the men whose names were presented to the Convention were: William H. Seward, of New York; Abraham Lincoln, of Illinois; Simon Cameron, of Pennsylvania; Edward Bates, of Missouri; William L. Dayton, of New Jersey; John L. McLean and Salmon P. Chase, of Ohio.

The Republican Convention to be held at St. Louis, June 16, 1896, will have presented for its votes all, or nearly all, the following names:

William McKinley, of Ohio.
Thomas B. Reed, of Maine.
Levi P. Morton, of New York.
William B. Allison, of Iowa.
Shelby M. Cullom, of Illinois.
Matt S. Quay, of Pennsylvania.
Charles F. Manderson, of Nebraska.

Among the prominent Democrats whose names will be presented before the Chicago Convention of July, 1896, are:

Grover Cleveland.
John G. Carlisle, of Kentucky.

William C. Whitney, of New York.
David B. Hill, of New York.
William E. Russell, of Massachusetts.
William R. Morrison, of Illinois.
Richard P. Bland.

If a Republican is to be placed at the helm of this grand union of States, we hope that one will be selected that will have the welfare of all the people at heart, as did Abraham Lincoln, the nominee of the Chicago Convention in 1860.

Mr. Lincoln called into his first Cabinet four of the candidates who were before the Convention for the Presidency—William H. Seward, Secretary of State; Simon Cameron, Secretary of War; Salmon P. Chase, Secretary of the Treasury; and Edward Bates, Attorney General. Caleb B. Smith, Secretary of the Interior, and Gideon Welles, Secretary of the Navy, took an active part in the Convention, and Montgomery Blair, Postmaster General, was not present.

Many of the prominent men who were in the Convention were rewarded with good appointments, although nearly all of them were in opposition to Mr. Lincoln during the balloting. William L. Dayton was sent as minister to France, Thomas Corwin to Mexico, N. B. Judd to Prussia, Cassius M. Clay to Russia, Carl Schurz to Spain, David K. Cartter to Bolivia, Frederick Hassaurek to Ecuador.

Among the men who figured prominently in the Convention, and afterward rose to distinction, are William M. Evarts, of New York; Senator David Davis, of Illinois, Senator and Justice of the Supreme Court; George S. Boutwell, Massachusetts, first Commissioner of Internal Revenue in 1862, and Secretary of the Treasury under Grant; F. P. Blair, Major General in the Union Army; Horace Greeley, editor "N. Y. Tribune;" Thaddeus Stevens, Penn., member of Congress; William D. Kelly, Penn., member of Congress; Thomas C. Fletcher, Mo., Governor; C. F. Clarkson, Iowa, member of Congress; Aaron F. Craigin, N. H., U. S. Senator; Columbus Delano, Ohio, Secretary of the Interior; Ben Wade, Ohio, U. S. Senator; Andrew G. Curtin, Penn., Governor; John A. Andrew, Mass., Governor; Edwin D. Morgan, N. Y., Governor; Austin Blair, Mich., Governor; B. Gratz Brown, Mo., Governor, and candidate for Vice President with Horace Greeley; Thurlow Weed, N. Y., journalist, etc., etc.

Abraham Lincoln was called to guide the ship of State that rocked on the turbulent waves of War, commencing soon after his election and lasting until he died in the fullness of his fame.

OSBORN H. OLDROYD.

Washington, D. C., 1896.

CHAPTER I.

Early Movements in Illinois for Lincoln.

The "Central Illinois Gazette," in 1859, hoisted the name of "Abe Lincoln" for the Presidency, with the following editorial:

"All men who have the success of the great cause at heart, and who are able to divest themselves of local feelings and personal predilections, seem to see clearly the force of the element of which his strength consists, and to recognize in him, in an unsurpassed degree, that availability which will be stronger than all other considerations in determining the Chicago nominations. With 'Old Abe' for President, and some sound and strong man from Pennsylvania or New Jersey for Vice President, the Republican party could carry the West in one unbroken sweep."

* * *

The "Chicago Press and Tribune" advanced the claims of Mr. Lincoln in the following article, February, 1860:

"Illinois claims that Mr. Lincoln, though without the ripe experience of Seward, the age and maturity of Bates and McLean, or the fire of Fessenden and Wade, has that rare and happy combination of qualities which, as a candidate, enables him to outrank either. The movement in his favor is spontaneous. He will enter upon the contest with no clogs, no embarrassment; and this fact is a guarantee of a glorious triumph.

"In all the fundamentals of Republicanism he is radical up to the limit to which the party, with due respect for the rights of the South, proposes to go. But nature has given him that wise conservatism which has made his actions and his expressed opinions so conform to the most mature sentiment of the country on this question of slavery, that no living man can put his finger on one of his speeches or any one of his public acts as a state legislator or as a member of Congress to which valid objection can be raised. His avoidance of extremes has not been the result of ambition which measures words or regulates acts, but the natural consequence of an equable nature and a mental constitution that is never off its balance.

"Mr. Lincoln is a man of the people. For his position he is not indebted to family influence, the partiality of friends, or the acts of the politician. All his early life a laborer in the field, in the saw-mill, as a boatman on the Wabash, Ohio and Mississippi, as a farmer in Illinois, he has that sympathy with the men who toil and vote that will make him strong. Later a valiant soldier in the Black Hawk War, a student in the law office, bending his great powers to overcome the defects of early training; then a legislator, and at last a brilliant advocate in the highest courts, and a popular leader of the great movements of the age, there is enough of romance and poetry in his life to fire all the land with shouting and song. Honest Old Abe! Himself an outgrowth of free institutions, He would die in the effort to preserve to others, unimpaired, the inestimable blessings by which he has been made a man."

* * *

The Sangamon County Republican Convention met at Springfield, April 28, 1860, and passed the following resolution:

"Resolved, That our distinguished fellow-citizen, the tall pioneer of Sangamon County, Abraham Lincoln, is our first choice for candidate for President of the United States; that we deem ourselves honored to be permitted to testify our personal knowledge, in every-day life, as friends and neighbors, of his inestimable worth as a private citizen, his faithful and able discharge of every public trust committed to his care, and the extraordinary natural gifts and brilliant attainments which have not only made his name a household word in the Prairie State, but also placed him among the wisest statesmen and most brilliant orators in the Union."

* * *

The Illinois State Republican Convention was held at Decatur, May 9 and 10, 1860. The "Illinois State Journal" of the next day narrates graphically the welcome given "Old Abe" by his fellow-citizens:

"No feature of the Republican State Convention was more clearly marked than the unanimity of sentiment which was manifest there for the Hon. Abraham Lincoln. The delegates from every part of the State vied with each other in exhibitions of their unbounded admiration for him. However they differed about other matters of party expediency—however they conflicted in their views about this or that candidate's claim for official honors—in 'glorious Old Abe' they found a common rallying point, and they joined hands and hearts with fervent zeal in awarding to him their distinguished consideration. In their speeches, in their conversations and in every act, they singled him out as the greatest popular champion of Republicanism, as the embodiment of their principles, and the extinguisher of Douglas doughfaceism in the State.

"Mr. Lincoln's presence in the 'Wigwam' as a spectator of the proceedings of the Convention was the occasion of a particularly interesting episode. He had, in pur-

ABE LINCOLN.
(Engraved from a Photo taken in 1860, and very much used in the Campaign.)

suance of the courtesy extended to him, hardly taken his seat upon the platform, amidst the wildest demonstrations of enthusiasm, when Mr. Oglesby, of Decatur, announced to the delegates that an old Democrat of Macon county, who had grown gray in the service of that party, desired to make a contribution to the Convention, and the offer being accepted, forthwith two old time fence rails, decorated with flags and streamers, were borne through the crowd into the Convention, bearing the inscription:

```
********************************************
*                                          *
*            ABRAHAM LINCOLN               *
*            The Rail Candidate            *
*           For President in 1860.         *
*           ──────────                     *
*    Two rails from a lot of 3,000 made    *
*    in 1830 by Thos. Hanks and Abe Lin-   *
*    coln—whose father was the first pio-  *
*    neer of Macon County.                 *
*                                          *
********************************************
```

"The effect was electrical. One spontaneous burst of applause went up from all parts of the 'Wigwam,' which grew more and more deafening as it was prolonged, and which did not wholly subside for ten or fifteen minutes after. The cheers upon cheers which rent the air could have been heard all over the adjacent country."

In that memorable Convention John M. Palmer (now U. S. Senator from Illinois) offered the following resolution, which was enthusiastically adopted:

"Resolved, That Abraham Lincoln is the choice of the Republican party of Illinois for the Presidency, and the delegates from this State are instructed to use all honorable means to secure his nomination by the Chicago Convention, and to vote as a unit for him."

CHAPTER II.

The National Democratic Convention, and the Secession from Its Ranks.

The National Democratic party met in Convention in Institute Hall, at Charleston, South Carolina, April 23, 1860. There was a full attendance of delegates from every State in the Union. Caleb Cushing was made Permanent President.

From Mr. Cushing's address we extract the following remarkable passage:

"Ours, gentlemen, is the motto inscribed on that scroll in the hands of the monumental statue of the great statesman of South Carolina, 'Truth, Justice and Constitution.' Opposed to us are those who labor to overthrow the Constitution under the false and insidious pretense of supporting it; those who are aiming to produce in this country a permanent sectional conspiracy—a traitorous sectional conspiracy, of one-half of the States of the Union against the other half; those who, impelled by the stupid and half insane spirit of faction and fanaticism, would hurry our land on to revolution and to civil war. These, the banded enemies of the Constitution, it is the part, the high and noble part, of the Democracy of the Union to withstand, to strike down and to conquer. Aye, that is our part, and we will do it in the name of our dear country—with the help of God we will do it; aye, we will do it; for, gentlemen, we will not distrust ourselves; we will not despair of the genius of our country; we will continue to repose with undoubting faith in the good providence of Almighty God."

On the fifth day the Committee on Platform reported to the Convention. A majority report was made on a platform which was adopted in committee by the slaveholding States and Oregon and California, and a minority report was made on a platform adopted by the Committee from the non-slaveholding States with the exception of Massachusetts. Benjamin F. Butler, of Massachusetts, presented a platform, besides several independent ones.

On the sixth day the Douglas minority platform was adopted by a vote of 165 to 138, whereupon the delegates from South Carolina, Alabama, Mississippi, Louisiana, Texas, Arkansas and Florida withdrew from the Convention. It was pretty generally understood at the beginning of the Convention that the Southern delegates would vote for no Northern candidate or Northern platform.

Here is the National Democratic (Douglas) platform:

"Resolved, That we, the Democracy of the Union, in Convention assembled, hereby declare our affirmance of the resolutions unanimously adopted and declared as a platform of principles by the Democratic Convention at Cincinnati in the year 1856, believing that Democratic principles are unchangeable in their nature when applied to the same subject matter, and we recommend as our only further resolutions the following:

"Inasmuch as differences of opinion exist in the Democratic party as to the nature and extent of the powers of a Territorial legislature, and as to the powers and duties of Congress, under the Constitution of the United States, over the institution of slavery within the Territories;

"2. That the Democratic party will abide by the decision of the Supreme Court of the United States on the questions of Constitutional law.

"3. That it is the duty of the United States to afford ample and complete protection to all its citizens, at home or abroad, and whether native or foreign born.

"4. That one of the necessities of the age, in a military, commercial and postal point of view, is speedy communication between the Atlantic and Pacific States, and the Democratic party pledge such constitutional government aid as will insure the construction of a railroad to the Pacific coast at the earliest practicable period.

"5. That the Democratic party is in favor of the acquisition of the island of Cuba, on such terms as shall be honorable to ourselves and just to Spain.

"6. That the enactments of State Legislatures to defeat the faithful execution of the Fugitive Slave Law are hostile in character, subversive of the Constitution and revolutionary in their effect.

"7. Resolved, That it is in accordance with the true interpretation of the Cincinnati platform, that, during the existence of the Territorial Governments, the measure of restriction, whatever it may be, imposed by the Federal Constitution on the power of the Territorial Legislature over the subject of the domestic relations, as the same has been, or shall hereafter be, finally determined by the Supreme Court of the United States, shall be respected by all good citizens, and enforced with promptness and fidelity by every branch of the General Government."

For three days the Convention balloted ineffectually for candidates, Douglas leading by 150 1-2 till the twenty-third ballot, when he gained two; on the thirty-sixth ballot he fell to 151 1-2, which he continued to poll until the fifty-seventh. Failing to nominate him by the necessary two-thirds vote the Convention adjourned in despair, on the 3rd of May and tenth day of the Convention, to meet in Baltimore on the 18th of June.

* * *

The Southern Seceders' Convention.

The Southern Seceders met in Convention at St. Andrew's Hall, Charleston, May 1st, and called John C. Preston, of South Carolina, to the chair, and he delivered the following address:

"We only know the imperiled institutions of our country, and we are here to preserve our rights and to redress our wrongs. If we had submitted quietly to the unjust proceedings of the Convention we have left, we should have done that which would have driven us from the land our forefathers gave us; we should have had denied to us the liberty they fought for; and ultimately we would have been driven from the spot in which their sacred ashes repose."

Mr. Yancey then took the floor, and gave his views on the position occupied by the Southern delegates:

"We appear here simply as citizens of the States in which we live. We were sent to the National Democratic Convention as delegates; but our mission has been fulfilled, and we retire as mere citizens from the late National Convention, for it is a mere sectional gathering. A few Southern delegates still remain there; but it is in the hope of being able to induce the majority to forego their black Republican purposes that I now propose that we shall take no action at present, but remain here to watch the proceedings of that body of which we were recently members. Should they nominate Stephen Arnold Douglas, it will then become our duty to present or recommend to the people of the United States candidates for President and Vice President of the United States on a fair, just and constitutional basis, and, therefore, a Southern basis. No action, however, should be taken by the seceding delegates until the proper time arrived."

The Convention adjourned to the Military Hall, where the roll call was answered by delegates from Florida, Alabama, Mississippi, Louisiana and Texas, the entire delegations from South Carolina and Arkansas with the exception of one vote. Georgia had twenty-six out of thirty-three, Delaware had two, and there were one each from Virginia and Missouri. James A. Bayard, of Delaware, was elected permanent Chairman.

On the second day the Convention adopted the following platform, which was the one reported by a majority of the Committee on Platform in the regular Convention:

"Resolved, That the platform adopted by the Democratic party at Cincinnati be affirmed, with the following explanatory resolutions:

"1. That the government of a territory organized by an act of Congress is provisional and temporary, and during its existence all citizens of the United States have an equal right to settle with their property in the territory, without their rights, either of person or property, being destroyed or impaired by Congressional or territorial legislation.

"2. That it is the duty of the Federal Government, in all its departments, to protect, when necessary, the rights of persons and property in the territory, and wherever else its constitutional authority extends.

"3. That when the settlers in a territory, having an adequate population, form a State constitution, in pursuance of law, the right of sovereignty commences, and being consummated by admission into the Union, they stand on an equal footing with the people of other States, and a State thus organized ought to be admitted into the Federal Union, whether its constitution prohibits or recognizes the institution of slavery.

"4. That the Democratic party are in favor of the acquisition of the island of Cuba, on such terms as shall be honorable to ourselves and just to Spain, at the earliest practicable moment.

"5. That the enactments of State Legislatures to defeat the faithful execution of the Fugitive Slave Law are hostile in character, subversive of the Constitution and revolutionary in their effect.

"6. That the Democracy of the United States recognize it as the imperative duty of this government to protect the naturalized citizen in all his rights, whether at home or in foreign lands, to the same extent as its native-born citizens.

"Whereas, One of the greatest necessities of the age, in a political, commercial, postal and military point of view, is a speedy communication between the Pacific and Atlantic coasts, therefore be it

"Resolved, That the Democratic party do hereby pledge themselves to use every means in their power to secure the passage of some bill, to the extent of the constitutional authority of Congress, for the construction of a Pacific Railroad from the Mississippi River to the Pacific Ocean, at the earliest practicable moment."

On the 3rd, the Convention assembled and Mr. Meek, from Alabama, moved that a committee be appointed to prepare an address giving the reasons for the course pursued. He further said that any Southern State that shall go into the Baltimore convention, goes in it as an approver of squatter-sovereign doctrines. Quite a prolonged debate took place upon this subject.

Mr. Bayard left the chair and addressed the Convention. He approved of the platform, but it was not in the language that he would prefer. He was unwilling to assent to the preparation of an address by a committee, which was to go forth to the country before he could have an opportunity of examining it. He could not trust any man or set of men, however able and patriotic they might be, to speak to the public for him. He desired the unity of the Democratic party, and was prepared to support their nominee if he should prove to be a truly National man. But he must ask the permission of the Convention to allow him to decline the position in which they had placed him, and to retire from the Convention.

Robert Scott, of Alabama, was then chosen President. A resolution providing that an address or narrative of the grounds on which the Southern States seceded from the National Convention be prepared and published, together with the proceedings of this Convention, was adopted, when the Convention adjourned to meet in Richmond, Va., June 11. One hundred guns were fired from several of the Southern cities, and enthusiastic meetings held in honor of the final withdrawal of the Southern States from the National Convention.

* * *

In accordance with the above resolution the seceding delegates assembled in the Metropolitan Hall, in Richmond, Va., on June 11. On the second day a son of John C. Calhoun reported, for permanent President, John Erwin, of Alabama. The Committee on Credentials reported delegates from Arkansas, Alabama, Texas, Louisiana, Mississippi, North Carolina, Florida, Georgia, the Second District of Tennessee and the Seventh District of Virginia. Mr. Baldwin, of New York, made an appeal for admission for his delegation, and all efforts to break him off were unavailing until a motion was made and carried to adjourn until the 21st.

* * *

DOUGLAS AND JOHNSON.
Democratic Candidates for President and Vice President.

* * *

The adjourned Charleston Democratic Convention (regular) met at Baltimore June 18 and lasted until the 23rd. The dissensions which marked the Convention at Charleston were renewed at Baltimore. The breach between the Northern and Southern Democrats was widened, and the feeling of partisan bitterness was renewed. When the Convention was about to proceed to ballot for President, Hon. Caleb Cushing, President of the Convention, after a brief speech, withdrew from the Convention. Governor David Todd, of Ohio, one of the Vice Presidents, then took the chair, amid tremendous applause from the Douglas men. The Convention then proceeded to nominate. On the first ballot Mr. Douglas received 176 1-2; Guthrie, 19; Dickinson, 1-2; Breckinridge, 7. The second ballot resulted as follows: Douglas, 173 1-2; scattering, 17 1-2. Mr. Hodge, of Virginia, asked to have another ballot in order that all might have another chance of voting, and that then, if any refused to vote, depriving the Convention of a two-thirds vote, he would move to declare Mr. Douglas the nominee. The Convention again balloted, resulting as follows: Douglas, 181; Breckinridge, 7 1-2; Guthrie, 5 1-2.

The President of the Convention said: "With heartfelt satisfaction, as presiding officer of this Convention, I declare Stephen A. Douglas, by unanimous vote, the candidate of the Democratic party of the Union for President of these United States, and may God, in His infinite mercy, protect him and the Union he represents."

The Convention rose, the long pent up feelings broke out in cheers, and the utmost enthusiasm prevailed inside the building. The band played in the gallery, and was greeted with great applause. A banner was displayed in the gallery with the motto "Pennsylvania will hold the arch firm;" another white banner was displayed on the floor with the words, "Pennsylvania is good for 40,000 majority for Douglas." (To show how little Convention enthusiasm can be relied upon, Pennsylvania went 59,000 for Lincoln!) A letter was read from Mr. Douglas, in which he said: "Whatever you may do in the premises will meet my hearty approval. But I conjure you to act with a single eye to the safety and welfare of the country, and without the slightest regard to my individual interests or aggrandizement."

Hon. Benjamin Fitzpatrick, of Alabama, was chosen as a candidate for Vice President, but, in a letter afterwards declined the honor, and on the 26th of June the National Democratic Committee selected Herschel V. Johnson, of Georgia, as the nominee in his place. The Convention adjourned on the 23rd.

* * *

The Convention of Southern Delegates seceding from the National Democratic Convention at Charleston, met in convention for the third time, in the Maryland Institute at Baltimore, at 11 o'clock, June 23, three-quarters of an hour after the Douglas Convention had adjourned sine die. Mr. Walker, of Alabama, made a report, presenting the name of Hon. Caleb Cushing (who had withdrawn from the Presidency of the Douglas Convention) for President of the Convention. The name of Mr. Cushing was received with cheers, and his nomination carried by acclamation. Mr. Loring, of Massachusetts, addressed the Convention, pledging Massachusetts to stand by the South in her struggle for Constitutional right,

BRECKINRIDGE AND LANE.
Southern Candidates for President and Vice President,

and placed in nomination John C. Breckinridge, of Kentucky, for President of the United States. The other nominations were: R. M. Hunter, of Virginia; Daniel S. Dickinson, of New York; Joseph Lane, of Oregon; Jefferson Davis, of Mississippi. The Mississippi delegation withdrew the name of Mr. Davis, and the names of Mr. Hunter and Mr. Lane were also withdrawn. An attempt was made to nominate without a ballot, but failed. When the vote was carried, the whole number of votes cast was 105, of which Mr. Breckinridge received 81 and Mr. Dickinson 24. The States casting their votes for Dickinson then withdrew his name, giving the full vote of the Convention, 105, for Breckinridge. Joseph Lane was nominated for Vice President on the first ballot, receiving 105 votes. Deafening calls were made for Mr. Yancey, who took the platform amidst cheers. He congratulated the Convention on the nomination of a representative of the State rights Democracy, who was prepared to maintain their rights and the Constitution. Mr. Cushing returned thanks, and congratulated the Convention both on platform and candidates, after which the Convention adjourned.

THE POLITICAL REVOLUTION OF 1860. 23

BELL AND EVERETT.
Union Candidates for President and Vice President.

CHAPTER III.

The Constitutional Union Convention.

The Constitutional Union Convention met in the First Presbyterian Church, corner of Fayette and North streets, Baltimore, Maryland, May 9, 1860, and in the afternoon of that day chose as its President, Washington Hunt, of New York, and designated one Vice President from each State, also eleven secretaries.

On the second day, the Committee on Business reported the following:

"Whereas, Experience has demonstrated that platforms adopted by the partisan Conventions of the country have had the effect to mislead and deceive the people, and at the same time to widen the political divisions of the country, by the creation and encouragement of geographical and sectional parties; therefore,

"Resolved, That it is both the part of patriotism and duty to recognize no political principle other than the Constitution of the country, the Union of the States, and the enforcement of the laws; and that, as the representatives of the Constitutional Union men of the country in National Convention assembled, we hereby pledge ourselves to maintain, protect and defend, separately and unitedly, these great principles of public liberty and national safety, against all enemies at home and abroad, believing that thereby peace may once more be restored to the country, the rights of the people of the States reestablished, and the Government again placed in that condition of justice, fraternity and equality which, under the example and Constitution of our fathers, has solemnly bound every citizen of the United States to maintain a more perfect union, establish justice, insure domestic tranquillity, provide for the common defense, promote the general welfare and secure the blessings of liberty to ourselves and our posterity."

This platform was adopted by acclamation, and John Bell, of Tennessee, was elected on the first ballot for candidate for President.

Mr. Henry, of Tennessee, a grandson of Patrick Henry, thanked the Convention in the name of Tennessee for the honor conferred on the State by the nomination of John Bell, whom he announced patriotic and above all sectionalism. His life has been devoted to the common good and common weal of all America. If elected, his administration would be pure, patriotic and Constitutional. But it was said he was too slow, too cautious. That was a merit possessed by the Father of his country. A cautious man held the helm of reason to control his conduct. For himself, he could have fought under no other banner than that which looked to the honor, glory and perpetuation of the Union. The Revolutionary blood that flowed in his veins must be his excuse for dwelling upon the preservation of the Union. What must be the result of internecine war? To be true to his section he must rally to the standard of his State, and his venerable brother in Iowa must in like manner be true to his section. Thus, brother would have to dye his hands in the blood of a brother. How horrible the idea.

Edward Everett, of Massachusetts, was nominated for Vice President. After a number of speeches were made endorsing the ticket nominated, the Convention adjourned.

LINCOLN AND HAMLIN.
Republican Candidates for President and Vice President.

CHAPTER IV.

The National Republican Convention.

At 12 o'clock noon, on Wednesday, the 16th of May, 1860, the National Republican Convention met in Chicago, Illinois.

The Convention was held in a large building on Lake street, called the "Wigwam," put up for the purpose. As soon as the doors were opened, the entire body of the Wigwam was solidly packed with men, the galleries being equally packed with ladies. There were not less than ten thousand persons in the building, while an immense crowd were unable to get inside.

Governor E. D. Morgan, of New York, Chairman of the National Republican Committee, called the Convention to order, read the call, and delivered the following address:

"Usage has made it my duty to take the preliminary step toward organizing the Convention—a Convention upon the proceedings of which, permit me to say, the most momentous results are depending. No body of men of equal number was ever clothed with greater responsibility than those now within the hearing of my voice. You do not need me to tell you, gentlemen, what the responsibility is. While one portion of the adherents of the National administration are endeavoring to insert a slave-code into the party platform, another portion exhibits its readiness to accomplish the same result through the action of the Supreme Court of the United States, willing, by the indication, to do indirectly that which, if done directly, would bring a blush even to the cheek of modern Democracy.

"While these and other stupendous wrongs, absolutely shocking to the moral sentiment of the country, are to be fastened upon the people by the party in power, if its leaders are able to bring the factious elements that compose it into any degree of unanimity, there seems left no ray of hope except in the good sense of this Convention.

"Let me, then, invoke you to act in a spirit of harmony, that by the dignity, the wisdom and the patriotism displayed here you may be enabled to enlist the hearts of the people, and to strengthen them in the faith that yours is the Constitutional party of the country, and the only Constitutional party; that you are actuated by principle, and that you will be guided by the light and by the example of the fathers of the republic."

Hon. David Wilmot, of Pennsylvania, the Temporary Chairman, on taking the chair, spoke as follows:

"A great sectional and aristocratic party, or interest, has for years dominated with a high hand over the political affairs of this country. That interest has wrested, and is now wresting, all the great powers of this government to the one object of the extension of slavery. It is our purpose, gentlemen, it is the mission of the Republican party and the basis of its organization, to resist this policy of a sectional interest. It is our mission to restore this government to its original policy, and place it again in that rank upon which our fathers organized and brought it into existence.

"The Constitution was not ordained and established for the purpose of extending slavery within the limits of this country; it was not ordained and established for the purpose of guaranteeing and securing that institution. Our fathers regarded slavery as a blot upon our country. They went down into their graves with the earnest hope and confident belief that but a few more years and that blot would be extinguished from our land. No, citizens! This republic was established for the purpose of securing the guarantees of liberty, of justice and righteousness to the people and to their posterity. That was the great object with which the Revolution was fought; these were the purposes for which the Union and the Constitution were formed. Slavery is sectional; liberty national. (Immense applause.)

"And, fellow-citizens, shall we, in building up this great Empire of ours, in fulfilling that high and sacred trust imposed upon us by our fathers—shall we support this blighting, this demoralizing institution throughout the vast extent of our border? (Voices, loudly, 'No!') Or shall we preserve this land as a free land to our posterity forever?"

Rev. Z. M. Humphrey, of the First Presbyterian Church of Chicago, then offered prayer, amid the profound silence of the vast audience.

The rules of the House of Representatives were adopted for the Convention.

The afternoon session was called to order at 5:15 p. m. The Committee on Permanent Organization reported the election of Hon. George Ashmun, of Massachusetts, as Permanent President. The President was conducted to the chair amid enthusiastic applause. He then addressed the Convention:

"Gentlemen of the Convention, Republicans, Americans:

"We have come here to-day at the call of our country, from widely separated homes, to fulfill a great and important duty. No ordinary call has brought us together; nothing but a momentous question would have called this vast multitude here to-day—nothing but deep sense of the danger into which our Government is fast running could have rallied the people thus in this city to-day for the purpose of rescuing the Government from the deep degradation into which it has fallen. (Loud applause.) We are here in the ordinary capacity as delegates of the people, to prepare for the formation and carrying on of a new administration, and with the help of

GEO. ASHMUN,
President of the Convention.

the people we will do it. (Applause.) No mere controversy about miserable abstractions has brought us here to-day; we have not come here on any idle question. The sacrifice which most of us have made in the extended journey, and in the time devoted to it, could have been made only upon some solemn call; and the stern look which I see on every face, and the earnest behavior which has been manifested in all the preliminary discussions, show full well that we will have a true and deep sense of the solemn obligation which is resting upon us. Gentlemen, it does not belong to me to make an extended address, but allow me to say that I think that I have a right here to-day, in the name of the American people, to declare that we impeach the Administration of our General Government of the highest crimes which can be committed against a Constitutional Government, against a free people and against humanity. (Prolonged cheers.) The catalogue of its crimes is not for me to recite. It is written upon every page of the history of the present Administration, and I care not how many paper-protests the President may send to the House of Representatives. (Laughter and applause.) We here will find out for him and his confederates not merely punishment, terrible and sure, but a remedy which shall be satisfactory."

THE OFFICERS OF THE CONVENTION.

PRESIDENT:

Hon. George Ashmun, of Massachusetts.

VICE PRESIDENTS:

California..............................A. A. Sargent
Connecticut.........................C. F. Cleveland
Delaware.................................John C. Clark
Iowa.......................................H. P. Scholte
Illinois..................................David Davis
Indiana...................................John Beard
Kentucky..........................W. D. Gallagher
Maine.............................Samuel F. Hersey
Maryland......................William L. Marshall

Massachusetts....................Ensign H. Kellogg
Michigan......................Thomas White Ferry
Minnesota......................... Aaron Goodrich
Missouri...........................Henry T. Blow
New York....................William Curtis Noyes
New Jersey...........................E. Y. Rogers
New Hampshire......................William Hoile
Ohio...........................George D. Burgess
Oregon...........................Joel Burlingame
Pennsylvania.....................Thaddeus Stevens
Rhode Island..................Rowland G. Hazzard
Texas.........................William T. Chandler
Vermont...........................William Hebard
Virginia...............................R. Crawford
Wisconsin......................... Hans Crocker
Nebraska...........................A. S. Paddock
Kansas..............................W. W. Ross
District of Columbia...............George Harrington

* * *

The Convention assembled in the Wigwam at 10 o'clock Thursday morning. Rev. W. W. Patton, of the First Congregational Church, Chicago, offered prayer. The President read a message from outside, asking for speakers to entertain the twenty thousand Republicans and their wives who were outside the building. Hon. Thomas Corwin, of Ohio, from the Committee on Order of Business, made the following report:

REPORT.

"Rule 1. Upon all subjects before the Convention, the States and Territories shall be called in the following manner: Maine, New Hampshire, Vermont, Massachusetts, Rhode Island, Connecticut, New York, New Jersey, Pennsylvania, Maryland, Delaware, Virginia, Kentucky, Ohio, Indiana, Missouri, Texas, Wisconsin, Iowa, California, Minnesota, Oregon, Kansas, Nebraska, District of Columbia.

"Rule 2. Four votes shall be cast by the delegates at large of each State, and each Congressional District shall be entitled to two votes. The votes of each delegation shall be reported by its chairman.

"Rule 3. The report of the Committee on Platform and Resolutions shall be acted upon before the Convention proceed to ballot for candidates for President and Vice President.

"Rule 4. Three hundred and four votes, being a majority of the whole number of votes when all the States of the Union are represented in this Convention, according to the rates of representation presented in Rule 2, shall be required to nominate the candidates of this Convention for the offices of President and Vice President.

"Rule 5. The rules of this Convention will be the rules of the House of Representatives, in so far as they are applicable and not inconsistent with the foregoing rules."

Mr. A. B. James, of New York, offered the following report:

"Before we proceed to act upon those rules, I wish to say that, when the committee met, there were but seventeen out of twenty-three members present; that the fourth rule which has been adopted was only adopted by one majority, and, as a member of that committee, I propose to offer a substitute, which I will read as follows:

" 'The minority of the Committee on Business and Rules propose the following amendment to the Fourth Rule, as a minority report:

" ' "Fourth. That a majority of the whole number of

votes represented in this Convention, according to the votes prescribed by the second rule, shall be required to nominate a candidate for President and Vice President." ' "

Mr. D. K. Cartter, of Ohio, moved that the consideration of the Report on Rules be postponed until the report from the Committee on Credentials was made. The Committee on Credentials reported the following as the votes of the States in the Convention:

California	8
Connecticut	12
Delaware	6
Iowa	32
Illinois	22
Indiana	26
Kentucky	24
Maine	16
Maryland	10
Massachusetts	26
Michigan	12
Minnesota	8
Missouri	18
New York	70
New Jersey	28
New Hampshire	10
Ohio	48
Oregon	5
Pennsylvania	54
Rhode Island	8
Texas	8
Vermont	10
Virginia	30

Wisconsin	10
Kansas	6
Nebraska	6
District of Columbia	4

A long discussion followed in regard to the delegates from some of the States named, and a roll of the States was called on the motion of Mr. Lowery, of Pennsylvania, to recommit the report to the Committee on Credentials. The vote of the States stood: Yes, 275 1-2; no, 172 1-2. The Convention then adjourned to meet at 3 o'clock.

* * *

The Convention reassembled at 3:15 p. m., and the President, upon taking the chair, suggested that there were outside of the building twice as many honest hearts and wise heads as there were within it, and they had requested him to invite Governor Randall to go out and favor them with his views. Mr. Tracy, of California, said Mr. Corwin had better go out with Governor Randall.

Mr. Benton, of New Hampshire, Chairman of the Committee on Credentials, reported that the committee found gentlemen entitled to seats in the following States, and each State to the following number of delegates:

States.	No. of Delegates.	No. of Electors.
Maine	16	8

New Hampshire	10	5
Vermont	10	5
Massachusetts	26	13
Rhode Island	8	4
Connecticut	12	6
New York	70	35
New Jersey	14	7
Pennsylvania	54	27
Maryland	11	8
Delaware	6	3
Virginia	23	15
Kentucky	26	12
Ohio	46	23
Indiana	26	13
Missouri	18	9
Michigan	12	6
Illinois	22	11
Wisconsin	10	5
Iowa	8	11
California	8	4
Minnesota	8	4
Oregon	5	3
Territories.		
Kansas	6	
Nebraska	6	
District of Columbia	2	

On motion of Mr. Corwin, the report of the Committee on Rules and the Order of Business was taken from the table. Rules 1, 2 and 3 were adopted, and the majority report of Rule 4 was amended by the substitution of the minority report as follows: "That the majority of the whole number of votes represented in this Convention, according to the ratio prescribed by the Indiana

Rule, shall be required to nominate candidates for President and Vice President." The vote stood 358 1-2 for the amendment and 94 1-2 against it.

Mr. William Jessup, of Pennsylvania, from the Com-

WM. H. SEWARD.

mittee on Platform and Resolutions, reported that the following resolution had been adopted with great unanimity, there being but one or two dissenting votes on several of the resolutions. The Convention then adopted them unanimously after several verbal amendments.

* * *

PLATFORM OF THE REPUBLICAN PARTY.

Adopted in Convention at Chicago, May 18, 1860.

"Resolved, That we, the delegated representatives of the Republican electors of the United States, in Convention assembled in discharge of the duty we owe to our constituents, and our country, unite in the following declarations:

"1. That the history of the Nation during the last four years has fully established the propriety and necessity of the organization and perpetuation of the Republican party; and that the causes which called it into existence are permanent in their nature, and now, more than ever before, demand its peaceful and Constitutional triumph.

"2. That the maintenance of the principles promulgated in the Declaration of Independence and embodied in the Federal Constitution, 'That all men are created equal; that they are endowed by their Creator with certain inalienable rights; that among these are life, liberty and the pursuit of happiness; and to secure these rights Governments are instituted among men, deriving their just powers from the consent of the governed,' is essential to the preservation of our Republican institutions; and that the Federal Constitution, the Rights of the States, and the Union of the States, must and shall be preserved.

"3. That to the Union of the States this nation owes its unprecedented increase in population, its surprising development of material resources, its rapid augmentation of wealth, its happiness at home and its honor abroad; and we hold in abhorrence all schemes for disunion, come from whatever source they may. And we congratulate the country that no Republican member of Congress has uttered or countenanced the threats of disunion so often made by Democratic members, without rebuke, and with applause from their political associates; and we denounce those threats of disunion, in case of a popular overthrow of their ascendency, as denying the vital principles of a free government, and as an avowal of contemplated treason, which it is the imperative duty of an indignant people sternly to rebuke and forever silence.

"4. That the maintenance inviolate of the Rights of the States, and especially the right of each State, to order and control its own domestic institutions according to its own judgment exclusively, is essential to that balance of powers on which the perfection and endurance of our political fabric depend; and we denounce the lawless invasion by armed force of the soil of any State or Territory, no matter under what pretext, as among the gravest of crimes.

"5. That the present Democratic administration has far exceeded our worst apprehensions in its measureless subserviency to the exactions of a sectional interest, as especially evinced in its desperate exertions to force the infamous Lecompton Constitution upon the protesting people of Kansas; in construing the personal relation between master and servant to involve an unqualified property in persons; in its attempted enforcement everywhere, on land and sea, through the intervention of Congress and of the Federal Courts, of the extreme pretensions of a purely local interest; and in its general and unvarying abuse of the power intrusted to it by a confiding people.

"6. That the people justly view with alarm the reckless extravagance which pervades every department of the

Federal Government; that a return to rigid economy and accountability is indispensable to arrest the systematic plunder of the public treasury by favored partisans; while the recent startling developments of fraud and corruptions at the Federal Metropolis, show that an entire change of administration is imperatively demanded.

"7. That the new dogma that the Constitution, of its own force, carries slavery into any or all of the Territories of the United States, is a dangerous political heresy, at variance with the explicit provisions of that instrument itself, with contemporaneous exposition, and with legislative and judicial precedent; is revolutionary in its tendency, and subversive of the peace and harmony of the country.

"8. That the normal condition of all the territory of the United States is that of freedom; that as our Republican fathers, when they had abolished slavery in all our national territory, ordained that 'no person should be deprived of life, liberty or property, without due process of law,' it becomes our duty, by legislation, whenever such legislation is necessary, to maintain this provision of the Constitution against all attempts to violate it; and we deny the authority of Congress, of a territorial legislature, or of any individuals, to give legal existence to slavery in any Territory of the United States.

"9. That we brand the recent reopening of the African slave trade, under the cover of our national flag, aided by perversions of judicial power, as a crime against humanity and a burning shame to our country and age; and we call upon Congress to take prompt and efficient measures for the total and final suppression of that execrable traffic.

"10. That in the recent vetoes, by the Federal Governors, of the acts of the Legislatures of Kansas and Nebraska, prohibiting slavery in those Territories, we find a practical illustration of the boasted Democratic principle of non-intervention and popular sovereignty embodied in the Kansas-Nebraska bill, and a demonstration of the deception and fraud involved therein.

"11. That Kansas should, of right, be immediately admitted as a State under the Constitution recently formed and adopted by her people, and accepted by the House of Representatives.

"12. That, while providing revenue for the support of the General Government by duties upon imports, sound policy requires such an adjustment of these imports as to encourage the development of the industrial interests of the whole country; and we commend that policy of national exchanges, which secures to the working men liberal wages, to agriculture remunerative prices, to mechanics and manufacturers an adequate reward for their skill, labor and enterprise, and to the nation commercial prosperity and independence.

"13. That we protest against any sale or alienation to others of the public lands held by actual settlers, and against any view of the Homestead policy which regards the settlers as paupers or suppliants for public bounty; and we demand the passage by Congress of the complete and satisfactory Homestead measure which has already passed the House.

"14. That the Republican party is opposed to any change in our Naturalization laws, or any State legislation by which the rights of citizenship hitherto accorded to immigrants from foreign lands shall be abridged or impaired; and in favor of giving a full and efficient protection to the rights of all classes of citizens, whether native or naturalized, both at home and abroad.

"15. The appropriations by Congress for river and harbor improvements of a national character, required for the accommodation and security of an existing commerce, are authorized by the Constitution, and justified by the obligation of Government to protect the lives and property of its citizens.

"16. That a railroad to the Pacific Ocean is imperatively demanded by the interests of the whole country; that the Federal Government ought to render immediate and efficient aid in its construction; and that, as preliminary thereto, a daily overland mail should be promptly established.

"17. Finally, having thus set forth our distinctive principles and views, we invite the co-operation of all citizens, however differing on other questions, who substantially agree with us in their affirmance and support."

Upon the adoption of the platform, the delegates and the whole of the vast audience rose to their feet in a transport of enthusiasm, the ladies waving their handkerchiefs and the gentlemen their hats, while for many minutes the tremendous cheers and shouts of applause continued, and again and again were renewed and repeated. As soon as order was restored, the President announced that there would be speaking in the Wigwam at night. Motions were made to proceed to ballot for a candidate for the Presidency, but lost, and the Convention adjourned until 10 o'clock Friday.

* * *

The Convention reassembled at 10 o'clock and prayer was offered by the Rev. M. Green, of Chicago.

Nominations being in order, Mr. William M. Evarts, of New York, said: "In the order of business before the Convention, sir, I take the liberty to name as a candidate to be nominated by this Convention for the office of President of the United States, William H. Seward." (Prolonged applause.)

Mr. N. B. Judd, of Illinois: "I desire, on behalf of the delegation from Illinois, to put in nomination, as a candidate for President of the United States, Abraham Lincoln, of Illinois." (Immense applause, oft repeated.)

Andrew H. Reeder, of Pennsylvania, nominated Simon Cameron, of Pennsylvania; and D. K. Cartter, of Ohio, placed in nomination Salmon P. Chase. Mr. Thomas H. Dudley, of New Jersey, presented the name of William L. Dayton.

Mr. Caleb B. Smith, of Indiana, seconded the nomination of Abraham Lincoln, of Illinois. (Tremendous applause.)

Mr. F. P. Blair, of Missouri, presented to the Convention the name of Edward Bates as a candidate for the Presidency. (Applause.)

Mr. Austin Blair, of Michigan, seconded the nomination for President of the United States of William H. Seward. (Applause.)

Hon. Thomas Corwin, of Ohio, presented the name of John McLean. (Applause.)

Mr. Carl Schurz, of Wisconsin, seconded the nomination of William H. Seward, of New York. (Applause.)

Mr. North, of Minnesota, seconded the nomination of William H. Seward. (Applause.)*

Mr. William A. Phillips, of Kansas, seconded the name of William H. Seward, of New York.

Mr. Columbus Delano, of Ohio, seconded the nomination of "the man who can split rails and maul Democrats"—Abraham Lincoln. (Great applause.)

Mr. Andrew, of Massachusetts, moved that the Convention proceed to vote.

The only names that produced really great applause were those Lincoln and Seward. Everybody felt that the fight was between them, and yelled accordingly. Murat Halstead describes the scene in a thrilling manner:

"The applause when Mr. Evarts named Seward was enthusiastic. When Mr. Judd named Lincoln the response was prodigious, rising and rising far above the Seward shriek. Presently, upon Caleb B. Smith seconding the nomination of Lincoln, the response was absolutely terrific. It now became the Seward men to make another effort, and, when Blair, of Michigan, seconded his nomination, the effect was startling. Hundreds of persons stopped their ears in pain. The shouting was absolutely frantic, shrill and wild. No Comanche, no panther ever struck a higher note, or gave screams with more infernal intensity. Looking from the stage over the vast amphitheater, nothing was to be seen below but thousands of hats—a black, mighty swarm of hats—flying with the velocity of hornets over a mass of human heads, most of the mouths of which were open. Above, all around the galleries, hats and handkerchiefs were flying in the tempest together. The wonder of the thing was that the Seward outside pressure should, so far from New York, be so powerful.

"Now the Lincoln men had to try again, and as Delano, of Ohio, seconded the nomination of Lincoln, the uproar was beyond description. I thought the Seward yell could not be surpassed; but the Lincoln boys were clearly ahead, and, feeling their victory, as there was a lull in the storm, took deep breaths all around, and gave a concentrated shriek that was positively awful, and accompanied it with stamping that made every plank and pillar in the building quiver."

We give herein the three ballots that were needed before the final, and glorious, choice was reached.

FIRST BALLOT.

STATES.	Wm. H. Seward, N. Y.	Abraham Lincoln, Ill.	Simon Cameron, Pa.	Edward Bates, Mo.	Salmon P. Chase, Ohio.	Wm. L. Dayton, N. J.	John McLean, Ohio.	Jacob Collamer, Vt.	Ben. F. Wade, Ohio.	Chas. Sumner, Mass.	John M. Reed, Pa.	Jno. C. Fremont, Cal.
Maine............	10	6										
New Hampshire.	1	7			1							1
Vermont.........								10				
Massachusetts ..	21	4										
Rhode Island....				1	1		5				1	
Connecticut......		2		7	2				1			
New York.......	70											
New Jersey......						14						
Pennsylvania....	1½	4	47½				1					
Maryland........	3			8								
Delaware.........				6								
Virginia.........	8	14	1									
Kentucky........	5	6			8		1		2	1		
Ohio.............		8			34		4					
Indiana		26										
Missouri				18								
Michigan.........	12											
Illinois..........		22										
Texas............	4			2								
Wisconsin........	10											
Iowa.............	12	2	1	1	1		1					
California.......	8											
Minnesota.......	8											
Oregon..........					5							
Territories:												
Kansas........	6											
Nebraska......	2	1	1		2							
D. of Columbia.	2											
	173½	102	50½	48	49	14	12	10	3	1	1	1

SECOND BALLOT.
Mr. Caleb B. Smith in the Chair.

STATES.	Wm. H. Seward	Abraham Lincoln	Salmon P. Chase	Edward Bates	Wm. L. Dayton	Jno. McLean	Cassius M. Clay	Simon Cameron
Maine	10	6						
New Hampshire	1	9						
Vermont		10						
Massachusetts	22	4						
Rhode Island		3	3			2		
Connecticut		4	2	4			2	
New York	70							
New Jersey	4				10			
Pennsylvania	2½	48				2½		1
Maryland	3			8				
Delaware		6						
Virginia	8	14						1
Kentucky	7	9	6					
Ohio		14	29			3		
Indiana		26						
Missouri				18				
Michigan	12							
Illinois		22						
Texas	6							
Wisconsin	10							
Iowa	2	5	½			½		
California	8							
Minnesota	8							
Oregon				5				
Territories:								
Kansas	6							
Nebraska	3	1	2					
District of Columbia	2							
	184½	181	42½	35	10	8	2	2

THIRD BALLOT.

STATES.	Abraham Lincoln	Wm. H. Seward	Salmon P. Chase	Edward Bates	John McLean	Wm. L. Dayton	Cassius M. Clay
Maine	6	10					
New Hampshire	9	1					
Vermont	10						
Massachusetts	8	18					
Rhode Island	5	1	1		1		
Connecticut	4	1	2	4			1
New York		70					
New Jersey	8	5				1	
Pennsylvania	52				2		
Maryland	9	2					
Delaware	6						
Virginia	14	8					
Kentucky	13	6	4				
Ohio	29		15		2		
Indiana	26						
Missouri				18			
Michigan		12					
Illinois	22						
Texas		6					
Wisconsin		10					
Iowa	5½	2	½				
California		8					
Minnesota		8					
Oregon	4	1					
Territories:							
Kansas		6					
Nebraska	1	3	2				
District of Columbia		2					
	231½	180	24½	22	5	1	1

THE CHOICE OF THE REPUBLICAN CONVENTION OF 1860.

The most intense interest was manifested as the balloting proceeded, especially toward the last, and before the result was announced, Mr. Cartter, of Ohio, said: "I arise, Mr. Chairman, to announce the change of four votes of Ohio from Mr. Chase to Mr. Lincoln."

This change gave Mr. Lincoln a majority of the entire vote, and Mr. Halstead says: "After a moment's silence, the nerves of the thousands, which through the hours of suspense, had been subjected to terrible tension, relaxed, and, as deep breaths of relief were taken, there was a noise in the Wigwam like the rush of a great wind in the van of a storm—and in another breath, the storm was there. There were thousands cheering with the energy of insanity. A man who had been on the roof, and was engaged in communicating the result of the ballotings to the mighty mass of outsiders, now demanded, by gestures at the skylight over the stage, to know what had happened; one of the secretaries, with a tally sheet in his hands, shouted: 'Fire the salute! Abe Lincoln is nominated.' As the cheering inside the Wigwam subsided, we could hear that outside, where the news of the nomination had just been announced. And the roar that was heard, like the breaking up of the fountains of the great deep, gave a new impulse to the enthusiasm inside. Then the thunder of the salute rose above the din, and the shouting was repeated with such tremendous fury that some discharges of the cannon were absolutely not heard by those on the stage. Puffs of smoke, drifting by the open doors, and the smell of gunpowder, told what was going on."

When partial silence had been restored, with many gentlemen striving to get the floor, Mr. Evarts, of New York, said: "Mr. Chairman, has the vote been declared?"

The Chairman answered: "No, sir."

Mr. Andrew, of Massachusetts, corrected the vote of his State so as to stand, 18 for Mr. Lincoln, and 8 for Mr. Seward; other States followed with changes. Half a dozen men were on their chairs making motions to the President, changing the votes of their States to Lincoln. Mr. William H. McCrillis declared Maine unanimous for Lincoln; Mr. A. H. Reeder, of Pennsylvania, announced 53 for Lincoln; Mr. Edward H. Rollins, of New Hampshire, 10 votes for Lincoln; Mr. Ames, of Rhode Island, 6 for Lincoln; Mr. Mills, of Connecticut, 8 for Lincoln; Mr. Cartter, of Ohio, gave the unanimous vote of 46 for Lincoln. B. Gratz Brown, of Missouri, cast the entire vote of his State for Abraham Lincoln. Iowa came in for a unanimous vote for Lincoln. Mr. Gallagher, of Kentucky, said he came not to obtrude, but to sanction the expression that was indicated, and cast a full vote for Lincoln. Mr. F. P. Tracy, of California, made the vote of that State 5 to 3 for Lincoln. The delegation from

Virginia made their vote unanimous for Lincoln. The Lone Star State of Texas wanted to record her full vote for Lincoln. The District of Columbia, with her two votes, changed to Lincoln. Mr. S. C. Wilder, of Kansas, said that he was authorized by the delegation to change the vote to the "gallant disciple of the irrepressible conflict, Abraham Lincoln." Nebraska followed with an entire vote for Lincoln. Oregon changed unanimously for Lincoln.

The Secretary then announced that the whole number of votes cast were 465; necessary to a choice, 234. For Abraham Lincoln, of Illinois, 364.

The Chair announced Abraham Lincoln as the candidate for President of the United States. This announcement brought forth thunders of applause.

Mr. William M. Evarts, Chairman of the New York delegation, said:

"Mr. President and gentlemen of the National Republican Convention: The State of New York, by a full delegation, with complete unanimity of purpose at home, came to this Convention, and presented as its choice one of its citizens who had served the State from boyhood up—who had labored for and loved it. We came from a great State, with, as we thought, a great statesman (cheers); and our love of the great Republic from which we are all delegates, the great American Union, and our love of the great Republican party of the Union, and our love of our statesman and candidate, made us think that we did our duty to the country, and the whole country, in expressing our preference and love for him. But, gentlemen, it was from Governor Seward that most of us learned to love Republican principles, and the Republican party. (Renewed cheers.) His fidelity to the country, the Constitution and the laws; his fidelity to the party, and the principle that the majority should govern; his interest in the advancement of our party to its victory that our country may rise to its true glory, induces me to assume to speak his sentiments, as I do—indeed the opinion of our delegation—when I move, as I do, that the nomination of Abraham Lincoln as the Republican candidate for the suffrage of the whole country for the office of Chief Magistrate of the American Union be made unanimous." (Enthusiastic cheers.)

The floor was accorded to Mr. Andrew, chairman of the Massachusetts delegation. He said:

"I am deputed, by the united voice of the Massachusetts delegation, to second the motion just proposed by the distinguished citizen of New York, that the nomination of Abraham Lincoln be made unanimous. Mr. President, and gentlemen, as we love the cause, and as we respect our own Convention, and as we mean to be faithful to the only organization on earth which is in the van of the cause of freedom, so do we, with entire fidelity of heart, with entire concurrence of judgment, with the firmest and most fixed purpose of our will, adopt the opinion of the majority of the Convention of delegates, to which the American people have assigned the duty of a selection; and, as Abraham Lincoln, of Illinois, is the choice of the National Republican Convention, Abraham Lincoln is at this moment the choice of the Republicans of Massachusetts. (Enthusiastic cheers.) We wheel into line as one man, and we will roll up our 100,000 majority, and we will give you our 13 electoral votes, and we will show you that this irrepressible conflict is the manifest destiny of the Democracy."

Mr. Carl Schurz then took the floor: "Mr. President, I am commissioned by the delegation of Wisconsin to second the motion made by the distinguished gentleman from New York. With the platform we adopted yesterday, and with the candidate who fairly represents it as Mr. Lincoln does, we defy all the passion and prejudice that may be enforced against us by our opponents."

Mr. Austin Blair, of Michigan, addressed the Convention: "Gentlemen of the Convention: Like my friend who has just taken his seat, the State of Michigan, from first to last, has cast her vote for the great statesman of New York; we shall now stand behind him in the great column which shall go out to battle for Abraham

Lincoln, of Illinois. Mark you, what has been obtained to-day, we will obtain in November next. Lincoln will be elected by the people. We say of our candidate, 'God bless his magnanimous soul.' (Tremendous cheering.) I promise you that in the State of Michigan, where the Republican party, from the day of its organization to this hour, never suffered a single defeat, we will give you, for the gallant son of Illinois, and the glorious standard-bearer of the West, a round twenty-five thousand majority."

Mr. O. H. Browning, of Illinois, said: "Mr. President and gentlemen of the Convention: On behalf of my delegation, I have been requested to make some proper response to the speeches that we have heard from our friends of the other States. Illinois ought hardly on this occasion to be expected to make a speech, or be called upon to do so. We are so much elated at present, that we are scarcely in condition to collect our own thoughts, or to express them intelligently to those who may listen to us. I desire to say, that, in this contest through which we have just passed, we have been actuated by no feeling of hostility to the illustrious statesman from New York, who was in competition with our own loved and gallant son. We were actuated solely by a desire for the certain advancement of Republicanism. The Republicans of Illinois, believing the principles of the Republican party are the same principles which embalmed the hearts and nerved the arms of our patriots of the Revolution, that they are the same principles which were vindicated upon every battlefield of American freedom, were actuated solely by the conviction that the triumph of these principles was necessary, not only to the salvation of the party, but to the perpetuation of the free institutions whose blessings we now enjoy; and we have struggled against the nomination of the illustrious statesman of New York, solely because we believe that we could go into battle here, on the prairies of Illinois, with more hope and more prospect of success under the leadership of our own noble son. No Republican who has a love of freedom in his heart, and who has marked the course of Governor Seward in the councils of our nation, who has witnessed the many occasions upon which he has risen to the very height of moral sublimity in his conflicts with the enemies of free institutions; no heart that has the love of freedom in it, and has witnessed these great conflicts of his, can do otherwise than venerate his name. On this occasion, I desire to say only that the hearts of the people of Illinois are to-day filled with emotions of gratification for which they have no utterance. We are not more overcome by the triumph of our noble Lincoln—loving him as we do; knowing the purity of his past life, the integrity of his character, his devotion to the principles of our party, and the gallantry with which we will be conducted through this contest—than we are by the magnanimity of our friends of the great and glorious State of New York in moving to make this nomination unanimous. On behalf of the delegation from Illinois, for the Republican party of this great and growing State, I return to all our friends, New York included, our heartfelt thanks and gratitude for the nomination of this Convention."

When at last the President announced the nomination of Abraham Lincoln, a scene of the wildest excitement followed. The immense multitude rose, and gave round after round of applause; ten thousand voices swelled into a roar so deafening that, for several minutes, every attempt to restore order was hopelessly vain. The multitude outside took up and re-echoed the cheers, making the scene of enthusiasm and excitement unparalleled in any similar gathering.

A man appeared in the hall bringing a large painting of Mr. Lincoln. The scene at this time beggars description; 10,000 people inside, and 20,000 outside, were yelling and shouting at once. The cannon sent forth roar after roar in quick succession. Delegates tore up the sticks and boards bearing the names of the several States, and waved them aloft over their heads, and the vast multitude before the platform were waving hats and handkerchiefs. The whole scene was one of the wildest enthusiasm.

* * *

The Convention adjourned till 5 o'clock p. m., when it reassembled, and was called to order by the President. The first business in order was balloting for a candidate for Vice President. Mr. S. C. Wilder, of Kansas, placed in nomination John Hickman, of Pennsylvania. Mr. Cartter, of Ohio, presented the name of Hannibal Hamlin, of Maine, which was followed by great cheering. Mr. Lewis, of Pennsylvania, seconded the nomination of John Hickman. Mr. Boutwell, of Massachusetts, presented the name of Nathaniel P. Banks, and was received with great applause. Mr. Caleb B. Smith, of Indiana, presented the name of Kentucky's gallant son, Cassius M. Clay. Mr. Andrew H. Reeder, of Pennsylvania, was nominated by Mr. Lowery.

The first ballot resulted in "no choice," the following votes being recorded:

```
Hannibal Hamlin..................194
Cassius M. Clay...................100 1-2
John Hickman..................... 57
Andrew W. Reeder................. 51
Nathaniel P. Banks............... 38 1-2
Scattering votes.................. 18
```

On the second ballot:

```
Hannibal Hamlin received......367 votes.
Cassius M. Clay      "      ...... 86   "
John Hickman         "      ...... 13   "
```

Mr. Andrew withdrew the vote of Massachusetts for N. P. Banks, and cast it for Mr. Hamlin; Mr. Kelly, of Pennsylvania, withdrew the name of Andrew H. Reeder. The President announced the result of the second ballot, and declared Hannibal Hamlin nominated as the candidate of the Republican party for Vice President.

Mr. Blakey, of Kentucky, "in behalf of that gallant son of freedom, Cassius M. Clay," moved that the nomination of Hannibal Hamlin be made unanimous. Caleb B. Smith, of Indiana, seconded the motion, and said: "I beg leave to state, that, in the opinion of the Republicans, there is no one of the many distinguished advocates of the Republican party, no one of that illustrious band who are contending for the principles of freedom, who is more endeared to the great heart of the Republicans of this country than Cassius M. Clay. It is a very easy matter for us who live upon soil untainted by slavery, who breathe the free air of States where the manacles of the slaves are never seen, and their wailings are never heard, to advocate the principles of the Republican party; but, gentlemen, to advocate those principles upon the soil of slavery itself, in the very face and shadows of their altars and false gods, requires a degree of moral heroism of which but few of us can boast. I have an assurance that this cause will triumph, and that the flag of freedom will wave in triumph over the land. Let me assure you, gentlemen, when that cause shall be borne aloft in triumph, and its glorious folds shall be expanded to the wings of Heaven, you will see inscribed upon its brightest fold, in characters of living light, the name of Cassius M. Clay. (Great applause.)

"We have now completed the great work for which we assembled here. We have presented to this country a ticket which will command the love and admiration of Republicans everywhere, and the respect and esteem of the entire country. (Applause.) With the gallant son of Illinois as our standard bearer; with the platform which we have adopted; with the distinguished Senator from Maine as the second in command, I feel that we stand upon a rock, and the gates of hell shall not prevail against it.

"In behalf of my friends of Indiana, I would say, that, in any efforts which we have made to secure the nomination of Abraham Lincoln, of Illinois, we have been animated by no feeling of animosity toward the distinguished son of New York, for in no single State of the Union is the name of William H. Seward more highly honored than in Indiana. (Applause.) We would not, if we could, pluck one leaf from the laurel that adorns his brow; we would not tarnish one letter in the history which will render his name illustrious in all coming time. It is not that we have loved Seward less, but because we loved the great Republican cause more. Thirty years ago, on the southern frontier of Indiana, might have been seen a humble, ragged boy, barefooted, driving his oxen through the mountains, and he has elevated himself to the pinnacle which now presents him as the candidate of this Convention. It is an illustration of that spirit of enterprise which characterizes the West, and every Western heart will throb with joy when the name of Lincoln shall be presented to them as the candidate of the Republican party." (Great and long continued applause.)

Mr. Wm. McCrillis, of Maine, then followed with a few remarks:

"Mr. President and Gentlemen of the Convention: I will detain you but a single moment. I wish, in the first place, to make an acknowledgment, in behalf of the people of Maine, for the honor that this Convention has conferred upon them by selecting one of her distinguished sons for the candidate for the office of Vice President of the United States. Mr. President, the people of Maine were the ardent admirers and friends of William H. Seward. (Applause.) They believe that the candidate which this Convention would nominate would surely be the next President of these United States, and they charged their delegation, that, above all things, they should select a man loyal to the spirit of free government, loyal to the principles upon which our fathers laid deep the foundation of the great empire, loyal to the Constitution, and loyal to the Union of these States. And, Mr. Chairman, they believe, that, in the person of William H. Seward, the great Senator of New York, all these great qualities combined, in addition to his eminent and distinguished services to the Republican cause, and his exalted statesmanship.

"Mr. President, and gentlemen of the Convention, however earnest we may have been in pressing the claims of our candidates, when the President of the Convention announced the result, all the partisan feelings and differences subsided, and we stood together as a band of brethren, as a united phalanx. And, when the electric spark shall convey the intelligence of the nomination to the remotest part of this Republic, every Republican will stand by his fellow, forming a united phalanx, and elect the nominee.

"Illinois and Maine are not only sisters under the Constitution—sisters-in-law, but they are by kindred and by blood. Of the people of New England, thousands upon thousands are our brethren and sisters who have emigrated to Illinois, and are scattered throughout the Great West. And here, sir, they are among the living, and here their bones repose among the dead. In 1856 the man who is now your candidate for the Vice Presidency of the United States, resigned his seat as Chairman of the Committee on Commerce in the United States Senate, and was nominated for Governor of the State of Maine. Maine led the van in the conflict. In September of that year, Maine electrified the nation by a vote of 20,000 majority. She was the Star that illuminated the whole Northern horizon; she was the Star of Hope—like the Star of Bethlehem. She came over and stood by the cause of freedom with her young and gallant leader. Mr. Chairman, I know the people of Maine well. I know that they will give a cordial and united support to this ticket; I know that, from every hill, from every valley, and every mountain—along her rivers, along her rock-bound coast—the nomination of Abraham Lincoln will be hailed with one spontaneous, loud, long and continued shout of enthusiasm and applause; that our people will inscribe on their banner, 'Lincoln and Hamlin;' 'Union and Victory.'" (Tumultuous applause.)

The motion to make the nomination of Mr. Hamlin unanimous was carried with the greatest enthusiasm. Loud calls were made for Tom Corwin; but Mr. Cartter informed the audience that he 'was lying ill at a private residence, but sent his full approbation of all that occurred,' and the assurance of his labor throughout the campaign.

Mr. Amos Tuck, of New Hampshire, offered the following resolution:

"Resolved, That the President of this Convention and

the Chairmen of the respective delegations be appointed a committee to notify Abraham Lincoln, of Illinois, and Hannibal Hamlin, of Maine, of their nomination by this Convention as candidates of the Republican party, for the offices, respectively, of President and Vice President of the United States." An amendment was made inserting 'unanimous' before 'nomination.'

Mr. Lane, of Indiana, was received with cheers.

"Freemen of the United States, you have to-day inaugurated a grand work. No event in the history of the United States, subsequent to the Declaration of Independence, is more sublime and impressive than the event which has this day been inaugurated in this vast presence of the freemen of the United States of America. Into your hands is placed the grand responsibility of bearing the torch of civilization in the vanguard of freedom. I ask you to bear it aloft and upward until the whole world shall glow with the light of our illumination. My fellow-citizens, the work commenced to-day shall go on until complete victory shall await our efforts in November.

"The position of many of the States of the West may have been misunderstood. We regard, to-day, William Seward as the grandest representative of the liberty-loving instincts of the human heart who exists in the United States. In our heart of hearts we love him, and would make him President to-day if we had the power so to do; but we regard Abraham Lincoln, of Illinois, as an equally orthodox representative of Republican principles, and a most beautiful illustration of the power of free institutions and the doctrine of free labor in the United States. In the present contest is involved not only the well-being, but the very existence, of the Government under which we live. I ask you by your action to sternly rebuke the disunion spirit which now disgraces the politics of the United States, and to turn hissing hot into the brazen front of Southern Democracy the brand of disunion, as God marked Cain, the first murderer. (Great applause.)

"My fellow-citizens, some doubts have been expressed in reference to Indiana. I pledge Indiana by ten thousand majority. (Great and enthusiastic applause.) I pledge my personal honor for the redemption of that State."

The roll was called, and each delegation appointed a member of the National Committee.

The thanks of the Convention were tendered to the President, Vice Presidents, and Secretaries, after which Mr. Sargent, of California, moved that the Convention adjourn sine die, when the President dismissed the meeting in these words:

"Gentlemen of the Convention: It becomes my duty to put to you the last motion which, in the order of parliamentary law, the President has the power to propose. It will probably be the last proposition which he can ever make to most of you in any Convention. But, before doing it, and before making a single other remark, I beg to tender you, each and all, my cordial thanks for the kind manner in which you have sustained me in the performance of the duties of this station. I confess to you, when I assumed it, I did it with some apprehension that I might not be able to come up to the expectations which had been formed. It was a bold undertaking in every respect, and I know that I could not have accomplished it half so well as I have done, but for the extreme generosity manifested on all sides of the house. There was a solemn purpose here, in the minds and in the hearts of not merely the Convention, but of the vast assemblage which has surrounded us, that, before we separated, we would accomplish a high duty. That duty, gentlemen, we have accomplished. Your sober judgment, your calm deliberations, after a comparison and discussion free, frank, brotherly and patriotic, have arrived at the conclusion at which the whole American people will arrive.

"Every symptom, every sign, every indication accompanying the Convention in all its stages, are a high assurance of success, and I will not doubt, and none of us doubt, that it will be a glorious success.

"Allow me to say of the nominees, that, although it may be of no consequence to the American people or to you, they are both personally known to me. It was my good fortune to have served with Mr. Lincoln in the Congress of the United States, and I rejoice in the opportunity to say that there was never elected to the House of Representatives a purer or a more intelligent and loyal Representative than Abraham Lincoln. (Great applause.) The contest through which he passed during the last two years has tried him as by fire, and in that contest in which we are about to go for him now, I am sure that there is not one man in this country that will be compelled to hang his head for anything in the life of Abraham Lincoln. You have a candidate worthy of the cause; you are pledged to his success; humanity is pledged to his success; the cause of free government is pledged to his success. The decree has gone forth that he shall succeed. (Tremendous applause.)

"I have served also in public life with Hannibal Hamlin. In the House of Representatives we were ranged on different sides. He was a firm Democrat of the old school, while I was as firmly, and perhaps too much so, a copy of the Webster school. But, as is known to many of the gentlemen who sit here before me to-day, there was always a sympathetic chord between him and me upon the question that has brought us here to-day. (Great applause.) And while the old division of party has crumbled away, and the force of circumstances has given rise to new issues, it is not strange that we are found battling together in the common cause. I say then, gentlemen, that you have got a ticket worthy of the cause, and worthy of the country.

"Now, gentlemen, that we have completed so well, so thoroughly, the great work that the people sent us here to do, let us adjourn to our several constituencies; and, thanks to God, who giveth the victory, we will triumph.

"No other motion is now in order, but that solemn one which must come to us all. Is it your pleasure that we now separate? As many as are in favor of the motion that this Convention do now adjourn sine die, say aye."

The Convention adjourned.

* * *

(From the Chicago "Press and Tribune.")

THE REPUBLICAN FLAG.

Tune—"The Star Spangled Banner."

O, say, have you heard from Chicago to-day,
  As the news has flashed onward from station to station;
O, what is the name that the winged lightnings say,
  The Republican choice for the head of the Nation?
      See that rocket's red glare,
      Soaring high in the air,
      And freemen rejoice
      For a victory there!

Is it Seward or Lincoln whose banner shall wave,
To lead on the hosts of the free and the brave?

Now hear you that sound as it comes on the wind?
Is it thunder, or cannon, that news is proclaiming?
'Tis the honest, the able, the giant of mind,
It is Lincoln, 'tis Lincoln! all hearts are exclaiming.
   The first blow is given,
   Our fetters unriven;
   The Union stands firm
   In the free light of Heaven.
And the flag of Republicans proudly may gleam,
For Lincoln and freedom, o'er mountain and stream.

And what is the name on its folds we decry;
Link'd with Lincoln, twin stars of our confederation;
It shines in our flag as it floats on the sky,
As the bright orb that Maine holds in high estimation,
   And the Hamlin of Maine,
   Without blemish or stain,
   With Lincoln, shall lead
   On to freedom again;
And the banner of Lincoln and Hamlin shall wave
O'er the land that Republicans rose up to save.

We'll drive back the minions who live on the spoil,
Who barter our birthrights to subserve their ambition;
We, the sons of free labor, free speech and free soil,
We will send them all back to their normal condition,
   That the laws of our land
   May with Liberty stand;
   While the voice of the free
   Is the only command.
Then the banner of Lincoln and Hamlin shall shine,
And the South be content with the compromise line.

And thus be it ever when freemen shall stand

>   Between their free soil and a slave institution;
>   Blest with Union and love may the Heaven rescued land
>   Praise the Power that upholds the beloved Constitution.
>   Then conquer we must,
>   For freedom is just;
>   On God and our country,
>   In Union we trust.
>   And the banner of Lincoln and Hamlin shall wave,
>   O'er the land that Republicans rose up to save.
>
>   —Wm. H. Stickney.

* * *

The following letter of Leonard Swett, addressed to Hon. Josiah H. Drummond, of Portland, Maine, was dated at Bloomington, Illinois, May 27, 1860, shortly after the nomination of Mr. Lincoln at Chicago, and describes the whole historical scene in graphic expressions worthy of perusal and preservation:

"I made the acquaintance of Mr. Lincoln early in the year 1849. Since then we have twice a year traveled over five counties, spending together most of the time from September until January, and from March until June, inclusive. Originally most of the lawyers did this, but lately one by one they have abandoned the circuit; and for perhaps five years Lincoln and myself have been the only ones who have habitually passed over the whole circuit. It seems to me I have tried 10,000 lawsuits with or against him. I know him as intimately as I have ever known any man in my life, perhaps more intimately, if possible, than I knew you when I left Waterville.

"I was with him the week before the Convention. In speaking of the propriety of his going to it, he said he was most too much of a candidate to go, and not quite enough to stay at home.

"Our delegation was instructed for him, but of the twenty-two votes in it, by incautiously selecting the men, there were eight who would gladly have gone for Seward. * * * The first thing after getting our headquarters was to have the delegation proper invite the co-operation of outsiders as though they were delegates. Thus we began. The first State approached was Indiana. She was about equally divided between Bates and McLean. Saturday, Sunday and Monday were spent upon her, when finally she came to us unitedly with twenty-six votes, and from that time acted efficiently with us.

"Seward came there with very nearly strength enough to nominate him, that is, men who intended to vote for him. Bates was the next strongest, but that element was an opposition to Seward, because he was not available in the doubtful States, and would, as we well knew, come to the winning man in opposition to him. Pennsylvania wanted Cameron, and insisted Seward would not carry that State. New Jersey wanted Dayton, and insisted Seward would not carry that State. So, the first point was gained, that is, the united assertion of the four doubtful States, Pennsylvania, New Jersey, Indiana and Illinois, that Seward would be defeated.

"We let Greeley run his Bates machine, but got most of them for a second choice. Our programme was to give Lincoln 100 votes on the first ballot, with a certain increase afterwards, so that in the Convention our fortunes might seem to be rising, and thus catch the doubtful. Vermont had agreed to give us her second vote, so had Delaware, New Hampshire, an increase. It all worked to a charm. After the first days we were aided by the arrival of at least 10,000 people from Central Illinois and Indiana.

"It was a part of the Seward plan to carry the Convention by outside pressure. Thursday the preliminary work was done. The friends of all parties Friday morning gathered to the capacious Wigwam. About 12,000 people were then inside and more out. A line of men were stationed on the roof, the nearest to the speaker's stand, catching from an open skylight the proceedings within and reporting to his next man, and so on to the man on the front of the building, who, with stentorian lungs, announced to the thousands in the street. Stores were closed, and, seemingly, the whole city was there.

"First, opening the war, was the nomination of Seward. It was greeted with a deafening shout, which, I confess, appalled us a little. Afterward, Bates, McLean, Cameron and Chase came with moderate applause. Then came Lincoln, and our people tested their lungs. We beat them a little. They manifested this by seconding the nomination of Seward, which gave them another chance. It was an improvement upon the first, and placed us in the background. Caleb B. Smith, of Indiana, then seconded the nomination of Lincoln, and the West came to the rescue. No mortal eye before saw such a scene. The idea of our Hoosiers and Suckers being outscreamed would have been as bad to them as the loss of their man. Five thousand people at once leaped to their seats, women not wanting in the number, and the wild yell made soft whisper breathing of all that had preceded. No language can describe it. A thousand steam whistles, ten acres of hotel gongs, a tribe of Comanches, headed by a choice vanguard from pandemonium, might have mingled in the scene unnoticed.

"This was not the most deliberate way of nominating a President, I will confess; but among other things, it had its weight, and I hope convinced the New York gentlemen that when they came West some other tactics must be resorted to.

"Our increase after the first ballot was a little more than we calculated. On the third the ground swell was irresistible, and bore our man through, and the shout from the Wigwam and the shout from the street, as the man from the top shouted 'Old Abe, hallelujah!' and the cannon with its mimic thunder, told the city and surroundings we had won.

"It was a glorious nomination. Seward could not have carried Illinois or Indiana; nothing is more certain than this. Our people, when they opposed Seward, did it from no other motive than for the reason that it lost us our State, our Senator Trumbull his place, and placed us under the ban of Loco Focoism for twenty years. We felt as though we could not endure this, and hence the earnest effort for Lincoln.

"The nomination saves us. We will sweep the whole Northwest. The nomination is from the people, and not the politicians. No pledges have been made, no mortgages executed, but Lincoln enters the field a free man. He will continue so until the day of the election. He is a pure-minded, honest man, whose ability is second to no one in the nation. In twenty years he has raised himself from the captaincy of a flatboat on the Mississippi to the captaincy of a great party in this nation, and when he shall be elected he will restore the government to its pristine purity."

* * *

I. N. Walker, of Indianapolis, Indiana, now Commander-in-Chief of the Grand Army of the Republic, attended the Convention at Chicago, and on the evening of the day of the nomination, went to McVicker's

Theater, and witnessed Laura Keene play "Our American Cousin." The portrait of Abraham Lincoln was displayed on canvas as the nominee of the Convention. On the night of April 14, 1865, Laura Keene was presenting the same play for the one thousandth night in Ford's Theater, Washington, D. C., and Abraham Lincoln was witnessing it, when John Wilkes Booth fired the fatal shot that ended this great and good man's life.

CHAPTER V.

Lincoln Apprised of His Nomination.

The news of Mr. Lincoln's nomination was received at his home (Springfield) at noon on Friday, May 18, 1860, a few minutes after it was made; and soon after its reception, arrangements were completed for a ratification meeting. One hundred guns were fired during the afternoon, the bells of the city rang, flags were flung to the breeze from many buildings, and sincere pleasure was pictured on the countenances of the Republicans over the nomination of their distinguished townsman, Mr. Lincoln.

Mr. Lincoln had been up in the telegraph office during the first and second ballots Friday morning. As soon as the second ballot was taken, and before it had been counted and announced by the Secretaries, Mr. Lincoln walked over to the "State Journal" office, on Sixth, between Washington and Jefferson streets. He was sitting there conversing, while the third ballot was being taken, when Mr. Cartter, of Ohio, announced the change of four votes, giving Lincoln a majority; and, before the great tumult of applause in the Wigwam was fairly begun, it was telegraphed to Springfield. Mr. Wilson, telegraph superintendent, who was in the office, instantly wrote on a scrap of paper: "Mr. Lincoln, you are nominated on the third ballot," and gave it to a boy, who ran with it to Mr. Lincoln. He took the paper in his hand and looked at it long and silently, not heeding the noisy exultation of all around; and then rising, and putting the note in his vest pocket, he quietly remarked: "There's a little woman down at our house who would like to hear this. I'll go down and tell her." The people of Springfield were delirious with joy and enthusiasm.

LINCOLN'S HOME IN SPRINGFIELD, ILLINOIS.

HOUSE IN WHICH LINCOLN DIED, WASHINGTON, D. C.

CHAPTER VI.

The Ratification of the Nominations at Lincoln's Home, and the Visit of the Committee from the Convention.

A large and enthusiastic crowd assembled in the State House at 8 o'clock on the evening of the nomination. Speeches were made by J. C. Conkling and George R. Weber. Every allusion to Mr. Lincoln was followed by deafening cheers, and the meeting throughout was the most enthusiastic that had taken place in the city for a long time.

The meeting adjourned at 9 o'clock; and the vast crowd, preceded by the Young America Band, immediately started for Mr. Lincoln's residence. Arriving in front of the house, the crowd made loud calls for Mr. Lincoln, and they were soon gratified by seeing the tall form in front of them. Mr. Lincoln's appearance was a signal for renewed applause. When the cheering subsided, Mr. Lincoln said that he did not suppose the honor of such a visit was intended particularly for himself, as a private

citizen, but rather as the representative of a great party;
and in reference to his position on the political questions
of the day he referred his numerous and enthusiastic
hearers to his previous public letters and speeches. His
speech brought forth loud applause. At the conclusion
of the speech, Mr. Lincoln said he would invite the whole
crowd into his house if it was large enough to hold them
(a voice cried out, "We will give you a larger one on the
4th of next March,") but, as it could not contain more than
a fraction of those who were in front of it, he would
merely invite as many as could find room. The house was
invaded by as many as could squeeze in, and all were given
the right hand of fellowship. The 18th day of May, 1860,
was a great day for the Republicans of Springfield.

* * *

The committee appointed by the National Republican Convention, consisting of Mr. George Ashmun, President, and the Chairmen of the respective delegations, to notify Mr. Lincoln of his nomination, arrived at Springfield on the Saturday evening after the Convention closed. A large number of delegates accompanied the committee, with the Pennsylvania Cameron Band. The committee were met at the depot of the Great Western Railroad by the "Springfield Lincoln Club," and a large crowd of citizens escorted them to the Chenery House. Cannons boomed, bonfires blazed, and rockets leaped high in the air, while many of the houses around the public square were illuminated. From the hotel the procession marched to the State House, where an enthusiastic meeting was held, and addressed by many distinguished gentlemen.

Having partaken of a bountiful supper, the delegates proceeded to the residence of Mr. Lincoln. Among the delegates composing the committee were many of the most distinguished men in the great Convention, such as William M. Evarts, the eloquent spokesman of the delegation from the Empire State; Judge William D. Kelly, of Pennsylvania, whose tall form and great eloquence excited so much attention; Mr. Andrew, of Massachusetts; George Ashmun, of Massachusetts, the President of the Convention, the bosom friend of Daniel Webster; Mr. Blakey, of Kentucky; the loud-voiced Cartter, of Ohio, who announced the four votes that gave Lincoln the nomination, and others. They reached Mr. Lincoln's house, a two-story frame dwelling, situated on South Eighth and Jackson streets, five blocks from the Public Square. As they were passing up the steps to the gate, two handsome lads, of seven and ten years, met them with a courteous "Good evening, gentlemen." "Are you Mr. Lincoln's son?" said Mr. Evarts. "Yes, sir," said the boy. "Then let's shake hands," and they began greeting him so warmly as to excite the attention of the younger one,

THE POLITICAL REVOLUTION OF 1860.

PARLOR IN LINCOLN'S HOUSE, SPRINGFIELD, ILL.

who had stood silently by the opposite gate post, and he sang out, "I'm a Lincoln, too."

Whereupon several delegates, amid much laughter, saluted the young Lincoln. All the delegates having finally entered the large double parlors on the north side of the house, Mr. Lincoln stood at the east end of the room, while Mr. Ashmun delivered the notification of his nomination in these words:

"I have, sir, the honor, on behalf of the gentlemen who are present, a committee appointed by the Republican Convention, recently assembled at Chicago, to discharge a most pleasant duty.

"I have come, sir, under a vote of instructions, to notify you that you have been selected by the Convention of Republicans, assembled at Chicago, as their candidate for President of the United States. The committee deem it not only respectful to yourself, but as appropriate to the important matter which they had in hand, that they should come in person and present to you the authentic evidence of the action of the Convention; and, sir, without any phrase which shall either be considered personally laudatory to yourself, or which shall have any reference to the principles involved in the questions which are connected with your nomination, I desire to present you the following letter, which has been prepared, and which informs you of the nomination; with it you'll find the platform of resolutions and sentiments which the Convention adopted; and, sir, at your convenience, we will be glad to receive from you such a response as it may be your pleasure to give us."

Mr. Lincoln, upon being handed the document, responded as follows:

"Mr. Chairman and gentlemen of the Committee, I tender you, and through you the Republican National Convention, and all the people represented in it, my profoundest thanks for the high honor done me, which you now formally announce.

"Deeply, and even painfully sensible of the great responsibility which is inseparable from that honor—a responsibility which I could almost wish had fallen upon some one of the far more eminent and experienced statesmen whose distinguished names were before the Convention, I shall, by your leave, consider more fully the resolutions of the Convention—denominated the Platform—and without unreasonable delay, respond to you, Mr. Chairman, in writing—not doubting now, that the platform will be found satisfactory and the nomination accepted.

"And now, I will not longer defer the pleasure of taking you, and each of you, by the hand."

The various members of the committee were there and then presented to Mr. Lincoln, who greeted each one cordially.

When Mr. Ashmun introduced tall Judge Kelly, of Pennsylvania, to Mr. Lincoln, they shook hands, each eying the other's ample proportions with genuine admiration, Lincoln, for once, standing erect as an Indian during the evening, and showing his tall form in its full dignity.

"What's your height?" inquired Lincoln. "Six feet; what is yours, Mr. Lincoln?" said Judge Kelly. "Six feet four," replied Lincoln. "Then," said Judge Kelly, "Pennsylvania bows to Illinois, my dear man. For years my heart has been aching for a President that I could look up to, and I have found him at last in the land where we thought there were none but little giants."

Mr. Lincoln bore himself during the evening with dignity and ease. His kindly and sincere manner, frank and honest expression, unaffected, pleasant conversation, soon made every one feel at home, and rendered the hour and a half which they spent with him one of great pleasure to the delegates.

The committee then retraced their steps to the hotel, returning to Chicago at midnight on the special train that brought them. During the evening a mass meeting was held in the State House, and addressed by Fred Hassaurek, of Cincinnati, Ohio; Mr. Cartter, of Ohio; Hon. Amos Tuck, of New Hampshire; Governor Boutwell, of Massachusetts; Judge William D. Kelly, of Philadelphia, and others. The speeches were full of enthusiasm, and the speakers all gave assurance of the final triumph of "Old Abe." It was a grand opening of the campaign, and the enthusiasm which attended this meeting and the Convention at Chicago, aroused the patriots all over the Union.

SPRINGFIELD ILLINOIS

[From the Daily Journal of the 9th.]

A Political Earthquake!

THE PRAIRIES ON FIRE FOR LINCOLN!

THE BIGGEST DEMONSTRATION EVER HELD IN THE WEST!

75,000 REPUBLICANS IN COUNCIL!

IMMENSE PROCESSION!

Speaking from Five Stands by Trumbull, Doolittle, Kellogg, Palmer, Browning, Gillespie, etc., etc.

MAGNIFICENT TORCHLIGHT PROCESSION AT NIGHT.

MEETINGS AT THE WIGWAM AND THE REPRESENTATIVES HALL.

CHAPTER VII.

Endorsing the Nominations of Lincoln and Hamlin.

The names of Lincoln and Hamlin were inscribed upon banners and flung to the breeze throughout the loyal North. In New York, Pennsylvania and Indiana, as well as in Illinois, the voice of the people went up in shouts of joy over the nomination of Lincoln and Hamlin. In Albany, N. Y., where the friends of Mr. Seward were so strong, a dispatch was sent on the evening of the day on which the nominations were made:

"Nine o'clock P. M.—The Republicans of this city are now fairly waked up, and the wildest excitement prevails in regard to the nomination of Lincoln. State street is a perfect sea of fire from burning tar barrels. The whole heavens are illuminated with a red glare, cannon are firing, music is playing, and the people are shouting on State street and Broadway."

In New York, two six-pounders were brought to the Park, and fired each a hundred times—one of them by order of the Republican General Committee, and the other under the patronage of private citizens. Besides these, the Central Committee ordered one hundred guns to be fired in Madison and Hamilton Squares respectively. In Mount Morris Square, also, a big gun was brought out, and a hundred rounds announced to the citizens the nomination of Lincoln and Hamlin. Great numbers of enthusiastic Republicans gathered in the squares, and the excitement was intense.

In Philadelphia, the Republicans opened their campaign by an immense mass meeting in Independence Square. Speeches were made from four stands by Senator Trumbull, of Illinois, and many other distinguished gentlemen. Ward processions marched to the Square with bands of music, fireworks, transparencies, rails, etc. Senator Cameron said in a speech at a ratification meeting at Harrisburg, Pennsylvania, that "Lincoln was perhaps less known in public life than others; but who, on all occasions, when demands have been made upon his zeal and patriotism, has borne himself more bravely and honorably? In regard to the great interests of Pennsylvania, the subject of protection to labor, his record is clear, emphatic and beyond suspicion. He will require no endorsement to convince the people of Pennsylvania that their interests will be perfectly secure in his hands. Himself a laborer in early life, he has struggled with adversity until he has reached the proud position he now occupies, by the single aid of a strong purpose, secured by an unyielding will; and it is not in the hearts of Pennsylvanians to doubt such a man."

At Washington, D. C., an enthusiastic ratification meeting was held—the first time such a meeting was held in that city.

* * *

The Republican press responded in grand style all over the country.

The "New York Evening Post" said:

"Men are thrown upon their own intrinsic manhood for their reliance, and it belongs to each one to become the architect of his own fortunes. This unlimited freedom of action, though it has produced some social evils, has produced much greater good; and we do not believe that there is a nation on the globe in which the masses of the people are so prosperous, so intelligent, and so contented as they are in this nation. What more striking illustration of its effects could we have, than the rise of Mr. Lincoln to his present importance in the eyes of the world? Is he not pre-eminently the child of our free institutions? A poor orphan without education or friends, by the labor of his hands, by the energy of his will, the manliness and probity of his character, he raises himself to fortune and fame; a powerful party, which contains, to say the least, as much virtue and intelligence as any other, assigns him, without intrigues or efforts of his own, the first place in its regards, making him the bearer of its standard in a momentous political conflict, and in a few months we may see the once friendless boy the occupant of the Presidential chair."

Here is a "New York Tribune" editorial on the same subject:

"Probably no attribute of our candidate will, after all, endear him so much to the popular heart as the conviction that he is emphatically one of the people. His manhood has not been compressed into the artificial track of society; but his great heart and vigorous intellect have been allowed a generous development amid his solitary struggles in the forest and the prairie. With vision unobscured by the mists of sophistry, he distinguishes at the first glance between what is true and what is false; and, with will and courage fortified by his life of hardship, he is not the man to shirk any responsibility, or to shrink from any opposition. Moreover, he is peculiarly one to win our confidence and affection. To know 'Honest Abe' is to love him; and his neighbors in the West, although voting for him to a man, will mourn the victory which is to deprive them of his presence."

* * *

The following report from a special correspondent of the "New York Herald, who visited Mr. Lincoln at his home in Springfield, Illinois, in August, 1860, will prove of the highest interest:

"Among all the candidates for the Presidency of the United States now in the field, Abraham Lincoln, of Illinois, seems to be regarded by the people here as the only one who presents the appearance, emphatically and literally, of the man of the people. Without ostentation, without reserve, without any of those exquisitely polite attentions one finds in the man of the world, and especially in the aspiring politician, nurtured in the patrician atmosphere of Washington, Lincoln both looks the man, acts the gentleman, and mirrors at once the keenness of the astute statesman and the firmness of the rigid executive officer. The people say they have long wanted a President free from the corrupt influences which a long official residence at the seat of government is calculated to entail; and, from what I have heard and seen, within the space of a few months, a majority of the people of the North, and not a few at the South, are satisfied that in Lincoln they have found a man who comes nearer to a representation of their ideas in this respect than any other named candidate.

"Lincoln is in the prime of life and vigor—as strong, as lithe and energetic as almost any public man of his age, and showing in his features, his movements and manners, his intellect, his knowledge of law, government and the organic rules that sway men and found systems, evidences that he cannot be easily swerved from a purpose he conceives just to his countrymen.

"After a pretty thorough investigation, I find that there is not a man in this region who says a word against the honesty of Abraham Lincoln. They like his sociability and his familiarity. He is universally regarded as a plain, unassuming man, possessing strong common sense, wedded to a quickness of perception that detects the right from the wrong and winnows the chaff from the wheat, whether the question be one of a legal character or the selection of a true man from an impostor. We have conversed with many gentlemen in prominent political positions, but to Abraham Lincoln must we accord the palm of frankness. He had no disguises. The subject of Southern slavery was touched upon, and Mr. Lincoln emphatically declared that it was his principle not to touch it where it exists, but to prevent its spread into Territories now free. He spoke of slavery as an institution that did not meet the universal sanction of the Southern people.

" 'Public opinion is not always private opinion,' he said; and, instancing Lamartine's account of the execution of Louis XVI., wherein it appeared, that, although the leading revolutionists were publicly obliged to declare in favor of that deed, many of them were privately opposed to it, he said that 'it was the same with many people in the South; they were obliged to sustain slavery, although they secretly abhorred the institution.' He would protect the South in its institutions as they exist, and said that Southerners did not comprehend the position of the Republicans in regard to slavery.

"'The Southern mind,' he said, 'was laboring under the delusion that the Republicans were to liberate the slaves.' He swept this assumption away by a decisive denial of its correctness. He said he would like to go South and talk to the Southerners on this topic, were it not that the minds of some were so inflamed against him that they would not listen to his reasoning.

"Mr. Lincoln's personal appearance has so often been described in the newspaper prints that it is unnecessary for me to enlarge upon it here; but, as a great deal has been said about his ugliness, I will say a word or two on that score. Men of the West may care for personal beauty in women; but, in a man, beauty constitutes a very small claim upon their regard. Lincoln, however, is not an ugly man. His features may appear rugged to the casual observer; but, when engaged in earnest and entertaining conversation, they assume an aspect at once pleasing and engaging. Many men called handsome by belles lack expression in their features when in conversation, whereas the man of genius telegraphs his mind to others not only by his language, but by the masculine charm of facial expression. Mr. Lincoln confesses that he believes he will be elected."

* * *

Here is an excellent extract from the "New York Tribune" of those momentous days:

"Some fastidious gentlemen appear to be a good deal

disturbed at the presentation made of the Republican candidate for the Presidency, as having once been a rail-splitter, and at the prominence and significancy given to that portion of his early life by the exhibition at public meetings of rails split by his hand.

"The title of 'rail-splitter' given to Mr. Lincoln is merely an emphatic way of stating that he rose from the class of men stigmatized by the slaveholding Senators as the 'mudsills' of society, and the introduction of such into public meetings and political processions is but an emblematical reminder of the same fact, so far as concerns Mr. Lincoln personally. The point intended to be made is, that, having risen from rail-splitting to be a prominent citizen of Illinois, and a candidate for the Presidency, there must be talent and capacity enough in him to qualify him for the discharge of the duties of that office. The main object, however, is an appeal, and, as it seems to us, a perfectly fair one, to the sympathy and the self-respect of that great body of voters who split rails or follow similar laborious employments.

"It is a striking presentation of that great principle of our Democratic system, that the highest offices of the government are open to all, however humble their origin, who, by the display of talent, probity, and public spirit, shall attract the favor and secure the confidence of their fellow-citizens. It is simply saying to the mass of the voters, 'Here is a man who can be trusted to uphold the great interests of free labor. He must know and understand those interests, he must sympathize with them, for he once was a laborer himself.'"

* * *

The Republicans of Washington, D. C., met on May 19, at the rooms of the Republican Association, and, with the Marine Band, marched to the residence of Hon. Hannibal Hamlin, at his Washington home, and calling him out, he addressed them as follows:

"You have come to pay a tribute to our standard bearer, who has been taken from the great West, where the Star of Empire is culminating, if it has not already culminated; a man of comprehensive and vigorous intellect, and fully equal to the position designated. The architect of his own fame and fortune, he comes to us most emphatically a representative man—not only a representative man as an able and earnest exponent of Republican principles, but as identified with the laboring and industrial classes. Having, from early life to the maturity of manhood, devoted himself to physical labor, he can, as he does, but feel a keener sense of the rights of labor. He stands before the country, too, with a high moral character, upon which even a suspicion has never breathed, and with a political integrity above reproach."

HANNIBAL HAMLIN.

CHAPTER VIII.

Letters of Acceptance.

The following are the letters of Abraham Lincoln and Hannibal Hamlin, accepting the nominations tendered to them by the Chicago Convention:

                        Springfield, Ill., May 23, 1860.

"Hon. John Ashmun, President of the Republican National Convention.

"Sir: I accept the nomination tendered me by the Convention over which you presided, and of which I am formally apprised in the letter of yourself and others, acting as a committee of the Convention for that purpose.

"The declaration of principles and sentiments which accompanies your letter, meets my approval; and it shall be my care not to violate or disregard it in any part.

"Imploring the assistance of Divine Providence, and with due regard to the views and feelings of all who were represented in the Convention, to the rights of all the States and Territories, and the people of the nation, to the inviolability of the Constitution, and the perpetual union, harmony and prosperity of all, I am most happy to co-operate for the practical success of the principles declared by the Convention.

"Your obliged friend and fellow-citizen,
"Abraham Lincoln."

"Washington, May 30th, 1860.
"Gentlemen: Your official communication of the 18th inst., informing me that the representatives of the Republican party of the United States, assembled at Chicago on that day, had by unanimous vote selected me as their candidate for the office of Vice President of the United States, has been received, together with the resolutions adopted by the Convention as its declaration of principles. Those resolutions enunciate clearly and forcibly the principles which unite us, and the objects proposed to be accomplished. They address themselves to all, and there is neither necessity nor propriety of my entering upon a discussion of them. They have the approval of my judgment, and by action of mine will be faithfully and cordially sustained. I am profoundly grateful to those with whom it is my pride and pleasure politically to operate, for the nomination so unexpectedly conferred; and I desire to tender, through you, to the members of the Convention, my sincere thanks for the confidence thus reposed in me.

"Should the nomination which I now accept be ratified by the people, and the duties devolve upon me of presiding over the Senate of the United States, it will be my earnest endeavor faithfully to discharge them, with a just regard for the rights of all. It is to be observed, in connection with the Republican Convention, that a paramount object with us, is to preserve the normal condition of our territorial domain, as homes for freemen. The able advocate and defender of Republican principles whom you have nominated for the highest place that can gratify the ambition of man, comes from a State which has been made what it is by special action in that respect of the good and wise men who founded our institutions. The rights of free labor have there been vindicated and maintained. The thrift and enterprise which has distinguished Illinois—one of the most flourishing States of the glorious West—we would see secured to all the Territories of the Union, and restore peace and harmony to the whole country by bringing back the government to what it was under the wise and patriotic men who created it. If the Republicans shall succeed in that object, as they hope to, they will be held in grateful remembrance by the busy and teeming millions of future ages.

"I am, very truly yours,

"H. Hamlin."

CHAPTER IX.

More Ratifications and Endorsements.

Speech of Carl Schurz at the ratification meeting at Milwaukee, Wisconsin, on the evening of May 30, 1860:

"I had the honor to be a member of that committee who were to carry to Mr. Lincoln the official announcement of his nomination. The enthusiasm with which we were received at Springfield was boundless. There we saw Mr. Lincoln's neighbors, and it became at once apparent that those who knew him best, loved and esteemed him most. (Cheers.) And when I saw Mr. Lincoln, for I had met him before in that memorable Senatorial campaign in Illinois, when he, as a man of true and profound convictions, although discountenanced and discouraged by many leading Republicans, who thought it good policy to let Mr. Douglas return to the Senate without opposition, threw himself forward for the imperiled purity of our principles, grasped with a bold hand the Republican banner, which was in danger of sinking into the mire of compromise and unnatural combinations, and held it up proudly aloft in one of the fiercest struggles the country ever witnessed. (Great applause.) I met him then, when he bearded the lion of demagogism in his den, when the brilliant sallies of his wit and sarcasm drew shouts of delight from the multitude, when the thunderbolts of his invective rattled triumphantly against the brazen front of Stephen A. Douglas (applause); when the lucid, unanswerable logic of his arguments inspired every patriotic heart with new confidence in the justice of our cause, and when, under his powerful blows, the large Democratic majority of Illinois dwindled down to nothing. There I saw him do what perhaps no other man in the nation would have done. There I learned to confide in the patriot and the defender of profound convictions, to esteem the statesman and to love the man. (Great applause.)

"And, now, I saw him again, surrounded by the committee of the National Convention, who had come to lay into his hands the highest honor and the greatest trust that a political party has to bestow—an honor which he had not craved and had hardly been sanguine enough to expect. There he stood silently listening to the address of our Chairman; his eyes downcast; in his soul, perhaps, a feeling of just pride struggling with the overawing consciousness of responsibility. Then he answered, thanking them for the honors bestowed upon him, and accepting the leadership in the great struggle, not with the exulting tone of one who has achieved a personal triumph; not with the pompous airs and artificial dignity of one who is conscious of standing upon the great stage of the world, but with that unaffected, modest simplicity of a man who is strong in the consciousness of his ability and his honest intention to do right. (Applause.)

"Many of those who now surrounded him had voted for other candidates in the Convention, and some, still laboring under a feeling of personal disappointment, had come there, not without some prejudice unfavorable to Mr. Lincoln. But when they saw a man who had worked his way from the humblest station in life to his present eminence, not by fast speculation or adventurous efforts, not by the wing of good luck, but by quiet, steady labor,

LINCOLN CAMPAIGN BADGES.

unswerving fidelity to principle and his private and public duties, by the vigor of his genius and the energy of his character—the man who had won the confidence of the people and was now lifted upon the shield of a great national party, not by ingenious combinations and adroit management, but by the popular instinct—unfettered by promises, unpledged to anybody, anything but the people and the welfare of our country, his hands free to carry out the honest dictates of his pure conscience, a life behind him, not only above reproach, but above suspicion, a problem before him, for the solution of which he was eminently fitted by the native virtues of his character, the high abilities of his mind, and a strong, honest purpose, they all felt, that with this pure and patriotic statesman, all those great qualities would return to the White House, which makes Republican government what it ought to be —a government founded upon virtue. (Enthusiastic cheers.) And an Eastern delegate, who had voted against him in the Convention, whispered to me in a tone of the highest satisfaction: 'Sir, we might have done a more daring thing, but we certainly could not have done a better thing.'" (Prolonged applause.)

* * *

From George D. Prentice, in the "Louisville Courier-Journal:"

"The Republican organs, by common consent, designate their candidate for the Presidency as 'Honest Old Abe.' We are by no means disposed to deny his right to the designation. We know him personally, and, however strongly we may condemn some of the doctrines to which he is committed, we have at no time seen reason to doubt his honesty. We believe that he has the good of his country at heart. This much we take the pleasure of saying in his behalf."

* * *

Mr. Andrew, the Chairman of the Massachusetts delegation, in a speech at Fanueil Hall, Boston, delivered after the nomination of Mr. Lincoln, gives the following as his impression of Mr. Lincoln:

"At Springfield we saw him, all there was of him (laughter), and it was not a difficult matter to catch a sight of that honest and intellectual face, for he stood like Saul among his brethren, above every other man. I tell you, fellow-citizens, that a man six feet four inches high is found seldom—except on a prairie. It is a way they have of looking up and peeping over, for they are always aspiring to look beyond the horizon. Do you ask who is Abraham Lincoln? No man who has read his speeches or perused his debates need ask that question. He is one of the leading men of all the West, as a counselor and barrister; standing first among his peers, as a citizen admired, loved and revered for all the virtues which become and which adorn a man. He has a countenance which bespeaks the benignity and beauty of a noble soul. My eyes were never feasted with the vision of a human face, in which more transparent honesty and more benignant kindness were combined with more of the intellect and firmness which belong to masculine humanity. I would trust my case with the honesty, and with the intellect, and with the heart, and with the brain of Abraham Lincoln as a lawyer, and I would trust my country's cause in the hands of Abraham Lincoln as its chief magistrate, while the wind blows and the water runs."

* * *

Hon. William L. Dayton, of New Jersey, said:

"There is something in having the impersonation of a candidate before us. I recollect about the time of the Chicago Convention, a stranger complaining of the fact that Mr. Lincoln was destitute of the graces; some neighbor, who knew him well, answered, 'You are right, sir; neither the schoolmaster nor the dancing-master had anything to do with making that man; God Almighty made Abraham Lincoln.'"

* * *

Resolution passed at the Republican ratification meeting held in Cooper Institute, New York, June 7:

"Resolved, That we with confidence challenge the closest investigation and scrutiny into the whole public and private life of Abraham Lincoln. Born in poverty and obscurity, he has by his own efforts raised himself from humble life to an eminence that may justly command the admiration of friend and foe. With ability that no man can gainsay or deny, with a firmness and decision of character that nothing can sway, with integrity that has never been questioned, with a record for freedom that bears no taint, and with a broad and comprehensive natural ability that will guard over and protect the whole Union, we will rally around him, support him, and triumphantly elect him to the high position the people have designated him to fill."

THE WAR DRUMS ARE BEATING.

Sung by the Glee Club at the ratification held in Cooper Institute, New York, June 7:

> The war drums are beating,
>   Prepare for the fight;
> The people are gathering
>   In strength and in might.
> Fling out your broad banner
>   Against the blue sky,
> With Lincoln and Hamlin
>   We'll conquer or die.

The clarion is sounding
  From inland to shore,
Your sword and your lances
  Must slumber no more;
The slave-driving millions,
  See how they fly;
With Lincoln and Hamlin
  We'll conquer or die.

March forth to the battle,
  All fearless and calm;
The strength of your spirit
  Throw into your arm;
With ballots for bullets,
  Let this be your cry,
With Lincoln and Hamlin
  We'll conquer or die!

CHAPTER X.

The Origin and Splendid Work of the Wide-Awakes of 1860.

The greatest feature of the campaign of 1860 was the great Army of Wide-Awakes, which originated in the city of Hartford, Connecticut. It was a Republican auxiliary, semi-military in character, but political in purpose, and grew to be a vast army of torch-bearers, which brilliantly illuminated the thoroughfares of the North during the campaign. The various Clubs marched in fine military order, each man carrying a swing torch, with a small American flag attached to the stick, bearing the names of Lincoln and Hamlin. The uniform of the privates was a black enameled circular cape, a glazed military fatigue cap, varying in colors to suit the various clubs. The officers carried colored lanterns, and their uniforms varied in color and style. The measured tread, steady step and unbroken lines spoke of attention to drill. Among many of the fantastic movements made while marching was the formation of a rail fence. This was done by marching in single file from one side of the road to the other in right and left oblique manner.

On the night of February 25, 1860, Hon. Cassius M. Clay addressed the citizens of Hartford, Connecticut, and he was escorted by a few enthusiastic young men, who borrowed torches from a fire company. In order to protect their clothes they procured some glazed oilcloth and cut it in the shape of capes, and threw it over their shoulders, and also covered their caps. The novelty of their appearance attracted considerable attention and drew forth the hearty plaudits of the public. On the 3rd of March following, a meeting of young men was called, and they there and then resolved to form a "Wide-Awake" club of fifty. Much fun was made of the uniform by the opposition press; but the movement spread like wildfire, and on the 27th of March a parade took place with two thousand in line. The Republicans from all parts of the North wrote to Hartford asking for information, method of organization and rules. Circulars and instructions were sent by the thousands, the Constitution consisting of fourteen articles, with a light infantry drill, according to Hardee. There were various clubs that differed a little from the Wide-Awakes, but they were essentially the same in their general organization and objects. The clubs

PROCESSION OF THE WIDE-AWAKE CLUB OF HARTFORD, CONNECTICUT, ON THURSDAY, JULY 26, 1860.
(From "Frank Leslie's Illustrated" Newspaper, Aug. 11, 1860.)

bore various names. The Republicans were called "Wide-Awakes," "Lincolnites," "The Rail Splitters," "The Rail Maulers," "Ever Ready's," "Young Men's Union Club," "Union League," "Union Sentinels," "The Minute Men."

Douglas and Johnson Clubs were known as "Little Giants" and "The Little Dougs."

"The Bell Ringers," "Clapperites," "Bell-Everetters" and "Constitutional Union Men" were the Bell and Everett organizations.

The "Chloroformers" were organized for the purpose of putting the Wide-Awakes to sleep.

* * *

Answers to invitations from the "Rail-Splitter Wide-Awakes," of Springfield, to various Wide-Awake Clubs of Illinois to attend the great Republican demonstration of August 8, 1860, from letters in the "Oldroyd Lincoln Memorial Collection:"

Alton, Ill., July 31, 1860.
"L. Rosette, Secretary Wide-Awakes, Springfield, Ill.

"I desire to say that about 280 Wide-Awakes will start from Alton on the morning of the 8th of August, to join you in a grand ratification meeting. You will hear from us again when our arrangements are completed. We expect to ship 800 live Republicans from here by special train.

"J. H. Underwood,
"Captain of Alton L. W. A. Club."

"Beardstown, Ill., August 1, 1860.

"To the Springfield Wide-Awakes, the Beardstown Wide-Awakes send greeting.

"Gentlemen: It is the earnest desire of the Republicans of Cass County to see such an assembling of the masses at Springfield on the 8th, as shall strike terror to the hearts of all opponents of our worthy standard bearer, 'Honest Old Abe,' and rekindle, within the bosom of his friends, fires of devotion, that shall, in the coming November, sweep from the political arena those twin sisters of iniquity, 'Squatter Sovereignty and Disunion.' We have made arrangements to go to Springfield in full force.

"Edw. E. Foster."

"Indianapolis, Ind., August 23, 1860.

"L. Rosette, Springfield, Ill.

"Dear Sir: Had I received your note as I should, we might have arranged to be at your grand rally. Abraham Lincoln, who, by his indomitable energy and honesty, has hewed out for himself a name and fame that kings might envy, having come up from the people, it makes him the Washington of 1860, and, as I believe, in the Providence of God, brought forward at this time to lead a free people back to the principles of the Fathers of this once free republic, and carry the flag of freedom triumphantly over every opposition to complete victory.

"Yours in the cause of free speech and free men, Lincoln and Hamlin,

"W. J. H. Robinson."

"Virginia, Ill., August 4, 1860.

"L. Rosette, Secretary Springfield Wide-Awake Club.

"Dear Sir: We will be in Springfield between 8 and 9 o'clock on Wednesday A. M. There will be 100 Wide-Awakes from Beardstown, who will come through this place, and we will join them. I suppose there will be 1,000 Abe Lincoln Republicans from old Cass County.

Hoping that you may have a grand time—one that will do credit to 'Old Abe,' and to the place in which he lives, I am, sir,

"Yours very truly,
"H. Theo. Thomas."

"Bloomington, August 7, 1860.
"L. Rosette, Secretary Wide-Awakes, Springfield, Ill.

"Sir: We shall be down on the 11 A. M. train to-morrow with some 125 torches, with Republican enthusiasm enough for 1,000. Old McLean will send from 500 to 1,000 delegates.

"Yours in the Republican cause for 'Old Abe,'
"S. B. Brown,
"Captain Bloomington Wide-Awake Club."

"Beardstown, August 3, 1860.
"L. Rosette, Esq.

"Dear Sir: Your invitation was accepted by our company. One hundred of them will march to Springfield, a distance of thirty miles, leaving here Tuesday morning with a band of martial music, camping at Pleasant Plains that night, and reach Springfield about 10 o'clock on Wednesday.

"F. M. Durand,
"Secretary Beardstown Wide-Awakes."

CHAPTER XI.

The Lincoln Demonstration at Springfield, Illinois, August 8, 1860.

From the "Illinois State Journal:"

"A veritable political earthquake passed over this part of the State on yesterday. We have no adequate words to describe what our eyes beheld. Never, we believe, in the history of the country was there a larger or more magnificent political demonstration than that which yesterday took place here at the home of Mr. Lincoln. Certainly nothing has ever occurred in the West which at all compares with it. Heretofore we have been in the habit of referring to the Harrison Convention, which met here in 1840, or to the Tippecanoe mass meeting, which shortly afterwards assembled at Cincinnati, as large meetings; but henceforth the Lincoln Rally of 1860 will be the standard of reference. For its extent, its numbers and its display, it makes a new era in the matter of political demonstrations, while, by its vastness and enthusiasm, it proves conclusively that the people of Illinois are heart and strength for Lincoln.

"Thousands upon thousands were here from all the central counties of the State. Wide-Awake clubs marched a distance of thirty miles, camping en route. The day was most favorable for the demonstration, and the streamers, flags, banners and mottoes, flung to the breeze in all directions, made a magnificent affair. The procession was eight miles long, and it was with great difficulty that the various delegations were brought into line. The column was headed with a large rolling ball, indicating the onward march of the Republican principles. The Springfield Woolen Mills was represented in the procession by an immense wagon containing a power loom, driven by a small steam engine. During the progress of the procession they made several yards of substantial jeans cloth, from which a pair of pantaloons for Mr. Lincoln were cut and made up. Numerous wagons represented the rail-splitting scenes.

"Christian County delegation consisted of 103 wagons and 1,200 people. Scott County sent 200 wagons. Tazewell County came in wagons to the number of 500. Spring Creek delegation consisted of 170 wagons, filled. Jersey County sent 120 wagons. Cotton Hill Township had a log wagon on wheels, with an old settler in front splitting rails. In the Williamsville delegation was an immense wagon drawn by twenty-three yoke of oxen. This wagon was a perfect medley of workshops—blacksmiths shoeing a horse, another making a shoe, wheelwright making a wheel, a gang of men splitting rails, carpenters, tinners, shoemakers, weavers, etc. In addition to the hundreds of delegations in wagons and on horseback, the railroads entering the city reported bringing 197 cars loaded with 14,500 persons.

"The procession reached the fair grounds about 2 o'clock p. m. Speeches were made from five stands by the following speakers: Judge Lyman Trumbull; Senator Doolittle, of Wisconsin; Hon. John Wilson, Commissioner of the Land Office under Mr. Fillmore; Hon. Joseph Gillespie, Hon. John M. Palmer, Hon. R. J. Oglesby, Hon O. H Browning and others.

"Mr. Lincoln was called for as he entered the grounds,

and made the following speech, after being carried from his carriage upon the shoulders of the people:

"'My fellow-citizens, I appear among you upon this occasion with no intention of making a speech. It has been my purpose, since I have been placed in my present position, to make no speeches. This assemblage having been drawn together at the place of my residence, it appeared to be the wish of those constituting this vast assembly to see me; and it is certainly my wish to see all of you. I appear upon the ground here at this time only for the purpose of affording myself the best opportunity of seeing you, and enabling you to see me.

"'I confess with gratitude, be it understood, that I did not suppose my appearance among you would create the tumult which I now witness. I am profoundly grateful for this manifestation of your feelings. I am grateful, because it is a tribute such as can be paid to no man as a man. It is the evidence that four years from this time you will give a like manifestation to the next man who is the representative of the truth on the questions that now agitate the public. And because you will then fight for this cause as you do now, or with even greater ardor than now, though I be dead and gone, I must profoundly and sincerely thank you. Having said this much, allow me now to say that it is my wish that you will hear this public discussion by others of our friends, who are present for the purpose of addressing you, and that you will kindly let me be silent.'

"At the conclusion of these remarks, Mr. Lincoln descended from the platform, and with difficulty made his way through the vast throng who eagerly pressed around to take him by the hand. By an adroit movement he escaped on horseback, while the crowd were besieging the carriage in which it was expected he would return to the city.

"In the evening there was a magnificent display of torchlights and fireworks generally."

CHAPTER XII.

The Adventures of a Lincoln Rail.

A Relic with an Interesting History. Presented by Governor Oglesby to a citizen of Kentucky, and now back again in Illinois.

"Forrest, Livingston County, Ill., June 1, 1874.
"To the Editor of the Inter-Ocean.

"Sir: Nothing since the days of the Rebellion, has called out such an expression of patriotism in our community as the exercises conducted in the Methodist Episcopal Church of this village on Sunday, the 31st ult., pursuant to the proclamation of Governor Beveridge, to observe the day in memory of our patriotic dead.

"The church had been handsomely decorated with evergreens, flowers, flags, mottoes, etc. After appropriate services during the day, the audience met in the evening, and a procession of young ladies filed up the main aisle of the church, bearing an elegant silk flag. These were followed by fourscore years, carrying a genuine Lincoln rail.

"The history of this particular rail runs briefly thus:

It was sent by Governor Oglesby, of Illinois, to the Hon. Allen A. Burton, of Kentucky, soon after the nomination of Mr. Lincoln by the National Republican Convention at Chicago, of which Convention both Mr. Oglesby and Mr. Burton were members, and Mr. B. an elector-at-large for Kentucky.

"It had been planned by a noted slave dealer to mob the rail when it should arrive at its destination; and on its arrival, the mob, headed by its leader, surrounded the express office to do the deed of fanatic villainy; but a few determined faces about the express wagon caused the men to halt, waver and then sneak away. The rail has stood guard in Mr. Burton's house for fourteen years; and on its leaving there a few days ago, for his new home, at Forrest, Ill., it was escorted to the railway station by a large procession of patriotic citizens to bid it good-bye on its return to its native state. Its adopted county, that would gladly have seen it mobbed fourteen years ago, is now Republican in its politics, and mourns the absence of this rail as the loss of a great apostle of political righteousness. During the Rebellion, Mr. Burton's house was alternately taken by the Federals and Rebels as officers' headquarters; and, although they spared nothing else, it so happened that the rail was comparatively undisturbed until the other day, on its leaving Lancaster, Ky., when it was considerably chipped by some of its more enthusiastic and less reverent friends, who declared that a piece of it was the next best thing after a splinter from the true cross. Four years ago, the rail, draped in mourning, figured conspicuously at meetings held in Kentucky to ratify the fifteenth constitutional amendment, and had been a prominent object at Republican gatherings held for various purposes since the war, and now remains here at Mr. Burton's home, whither he has removed, as a reminder of what he suffered during the late war in behalf of the Union. Accompanying this rail is the following certificate:

"'Decatur, Ill., June 1, 1860.

"'I do hereby certify that the rail this day delivered to Dr. G. W. McMellen, to be by him sent to A. A. Burton, of Lancaster, Ky., is from a lot of 30,000 made by Abraham Lincoln and myself thirty years ago in this county, and I have resided in this county ever since that time.

"'His
'"John X Hanks.
"'Mark.

"'Attest: R. J. Oglesby.'"

"Forrest, Ill., March 22, 1888.

"O. H. Oldroyd, Esq., Lincoln Homestead, Springfield, Ill.

"Dear Sir: We send you the Lincoln rail that was sent to Judge Burton in 1860. Its history is given in the accompanying paper up to 1874. It has stood guard in

Mr. Burton's new home in Illinois since that time till now. This we send you is the identical rail with John Hanks' certificate, making it fourteen years since it was sent from Kentucky, and twenty-eight years in Mr. Burton's family.

"Lydia Burton Hurt.

"Nathan Hurt.

"Attest: Henry B. Watson."

Bless me this is pleasant riding on a rail

CHAPTER XIII.

Leonard W. Volk's Bust of Lincoln, from Life Casts of Face and Hands.

The bust of Lincoln by Leonard W. Volk, the well-known sculptor, of Chicago—a photograph of which will be found in the front part of this book—was made from sittings obtained in 1860, and with the assistance of life mask and casts of the hands also made by Mr. Volk the same year. The story of how Mr. Volk obtained the sittings for this bust and hand casts, is an interesting one, and was related by the artist in an article which appeared in the "Century Magazine" for December, 1881.

Mr. Volk had obtained sittings for a bust of Stephen A. Douglas in 1857, during the memorable Senatorial contest in Illinois between Douglas and Lincoln. He was accompanying Mr. Douglas on a speechmaking tour when he first met Lincoln at the town of Lincoln, in Logan County. A mutual friend introduced him. "How do you do? I am glad to see you. I have read of you in the papers. You are making a statue of Judge Douglas for Governor Matteson's new house," was Lincoln's greeting.

"Yes, sir," Mr. Volk replied; "and some time when you are in Chicago and have time, I should like to have you sit to me for your bust."

"I will, Mr. Volk," said Lincoln; "I shall be glad to, the first opportunity I have."

Nearly two years had elapsed when that opportunity came. Lincoln was in Chicago trying a case in the United States Court, and Volk, seeing his name in the morning "Tribune," called there immediately. Mr. Lincoln recognized him at once, and came to greet him. He seemed pleased at being reminded of his promise to sit for a bust, and asked when he should come to the studio, and how long he would be wanted at each sitting. It was arranged that Mr. Lincoln should come early every morning, and remain until 10 o'clock, the hour court opened. It was the first time Mr. Lincoln sat to an artist for his portrait in sculpture or painting; he had only posed before for daguerreotypes and photographs. Friday morning he had his first sitting, and the cast was made of his face. He came on seven succeeding mornings, while Mr. Volk made the clay bust, which was the model for the famous Lincoln beardless bust. On May 18th following, Mr. Lincoln was nominated for the Presidency by the Republican Convention in Chicago. Having occasion to go to

Springfield the day of the nomination, Mr. Volk called upon Lincoln at his home, and was the first Chicagoan to congratulate him upon his nomination. The sculptor made an engagement for a sitting on the second day following (Sunday) to obtain casts of Lincoln's hands. Saturday afternoon the committee appointed to inform Lincoln of his nomination arrived at Springfield, accompanied by a trainload of enthusiastic citizens. This crowd, swelled to thousands by the Springfield populace, marched to Lincoln's home; and, after the committee had performed its duties, they passed through the house in single file, each being allowed to shake Lincoln's hand as the line moved through. The cast of the right hand, made next morning, shows the effect, in swollen muscles, of this continued handshaking. When the sculptor was making the cast of the left hand, Lincoln called his attention to a scar on his thumb. "You have heard me called the rail splitter, haven't you?" he said. "Well, I used to split rails when I was a young man, and one day, while sharpening a wedge on a log, the ax glanced and nearly took my thumb off, and that is the scar left." The scar is plainly seen in Mr. Volk's cast.

CHAPTER XIV.

Two Great Speeches by Seward and Schenck.

Speech of William H. Seward, at Springfield, Illinois, October 1, 1860.

As the train bearing Mr. Seward and party arrived at Springfield from St. Louis, Missouri, Mr. Lincoln, with a large crowd of citizens, met them at the depot. A salute was fired as the train stopped. The correspondent of the "New York Herald" gives the following description of the few minutes' stay:

"Mr. Lincoln's portraits bear a sufficient resemblance to him to make recognition easy, and yet he is not by any means so hard featured and repulsive looking as they represent him. On the contrary, while no one would call him a good-looking man, neither would anyone be repelled by his aspect. The good-humored expression that lurks about his clear gray eye, traveling the one long, deep, curved furrow down his cheek, and making its home somewhere in the region of his capacious mouth, must always gain him friends. He dresses in the ordinary style of Western lawyers, black cloth swallow-tailed coat, and trousers fitting tightly to his long, bony frame; the inevitable black satin vest, open low down, and displaying a broad field of shirt bosom, the collar being turned down over a black silk neckerchief."

Mr. Seward spoke from the platform as follows: "I am happy to express, on behalf of the party with whom I am traveling, our gratitude and acknowledgments for this kind and generous reception at the home of your distinguished fellow-citizen, our excellent and honored candidate for the Chief Magistracy of the United States. If there is in any part of the country a deeper interest felt in his election than there is in any other part, it must of course be here, where he has lived a life of usefulness; where he is surrounded by the companions of his labors and of his public services. We are happy to report to you, that, although we have traveled over a large part of the country, we have found no doubtful states. You would naturally expect that I should say something about the temper and disposition of the State of New York. The State of New York will give a generous and cheerful and effective support to your neighbor—Abraham Lincoln. I have heard about combinations and coalitions there, and I have been urged from the beginning to abandon this journey and turn back on my footsteps. Whenever I shall find any reason to suspect that the majority which the State of New York will give for the Republican Candidate will be less than 60,000 (cheers) I may do so. The State of New York never fails—never flinches. She has been committed from the beginning, as she will be to the end, under all circumstances, to the great principles of the Republican party. She voted to establish this a land of freedom for you in 1787. She sustained the ordinance of 1787 till you were able to take care of yourselves. Among the first acts of her government she abolished slavery for herself; she has known nothing of compromises, nothing of conditions or qualifications in this great principle, and she never will. She will sustain your distinguished neighbor because she knows that he is true to his great principle; and, when she has helped to elect him, by giving as large a majority as can be given by any half dozen other States, then you will find that she will ask less, expect less, from him, and support him more faithfully than any other State can do. That is the way she did with John Quincy Adams, that is the way she sustained General Taylor, and that is the way she will sustain Lincoln."

Mr. Seward was loudly cheered as the train swept on.

* * *

Speech of Robert E. Schenck at the Stuyvesant Institute, New York, September, 1860.

"My Fellow-Citizens of New York: I know Mr. Lincoln—this Western candidate whom we have presented

to you, whom you and we have chosen to be our standard
bearer in this battle for freedom, for the Constitution,
and the Union, as they were understood and expressed
by our fathers—this leader of the host, with whom we
would march back and intrench ourselves in the old and
sure strongholds of that sound interpretation of our organic law, and that wholesome and wise practice and
policy which were established and maintained so long by
the great men who have gone before us. I know him. It
was my fortune to sit beside him for two years while he
served in the councils of the nation, and until he had to
decline, out of consideration for his personal duties and
necessities, a longer term in the public service. It has
since been my pride to continue the friendly relations then
formed through the years that have since passed. Modest and unobtrusive in his manner, yet in the short period
of that service, and with such opportunity of acquaintance
and observation, it was not possible to fail to see that he
was a man of no ordinary stamp—one that might yet
make his mark higher and more conspicuously; one that,
by his clear, logical intellect, his forceful power of argu-
mentation, his fair, straightforward course, and his manifest, influencing honesty of purpose, would prove himself, on trial at any time, if need be, worthy of and compe-
tent for any station or trust, however high or responsible,
to which he might be called. And these are the qualities

of mind and character peculiarly needed in him who is to be put at the head of the Nation at this crisis of our public affairs."

BANNER PAINTED BY REUBEN NEAL LAWRENCE.

CHAPTER XV.

A Pen Picture of Abraham Lincoln.

Correspondence of the Philadelphia "North American:"

"Springfield, Ill., October 20, 1860.

"So much has been written and spoken of Abraham Lincoln, the next President of the United States, that the public mind is already reasonably possessed, from various descriptions, good, bad and indifferent, as well as by the never-failing popular instinct, of his general characteristics, appearance and bearing. The ordinary likenesses do his face and features much injustice, while they still convey that important idea of both which makes recognition easy and certain. I had not met him until yesterday in thirteen years, since he left Congress, where his name was uniformly recorded on the Whig side, and where he was always recognized as one of our most staunch and reliable champions. Time has touched him with a gentle hand, and he is to-day the same open and ingenuous gentleman that he was regarded by a large circle of admiring friends in that memorable period, and when the Senate and the House of Representatives numbered some of the foremost intellects of the Nation.

"Mr. Lincoln may be regarded as representing what I will venture to call the highest type of Western civilization in this country; for the development of manhood west of the Ohio is essentially different from what we are accustomed to see east of it. He is, in other words, a representative of that energetic sturdy and progressive people, who have, by their own strong arms and stout hearts, cleared the forests, plowed the prairies, constructed the railroads and carried the churches and school-houses into the once wilderness of this mighty region, causing it to blossom like a garden, and diffusing blessings everywhere. We have a right to be fond of the West, for there is no known spot on the habitable globe which to-day exhibits the same wonderful progress, or gives promise of such future greatness. And if this feeling of National pride be proper, as every American must feel it to be, with how much honorable consciousness can we point to our candidate, who personates, as it were, those remarkable qualities, and claim for him the suffrage of the people.

"However politics may separate partialities in this State, there is but one opinion among fair-minded men as to the moral worth, elevated character and purity of Abraham Lincoln. In Springfield, which has been so long his home, all parties vie with each other in testifying to his integrity, his uprightness and all the virtues which adorn and dignify private life.

"In his intercourse he is frank, direct and manly, without reservations or quibblings of any kind. While maintaining a decorous and delicate reserve in regard to that immediate future which is now foreshadowed so unmistakably, he is entirely free to express his opinions on all subjects of public policy, and particularly in regard to the great principles which have of late years so much divided the parties. Mr. Lincoln stands nearer to the old and recognized landmarks of the Constitution, which have been honored of all men, than almost any public man now before the country. He is eminently and necessarily conservative in regard to slavery, from conviction, from long reflection, from all his previous life, and from the firm persuasion that moderation is the only course by which this government can be administered wisely and well.

"Opinion in this region is nearly identical with that entertained in Philadelphia on this exciting question, and it may be said to extend along the great belt to the Atlantic, including a population of eight or more millions.

"The administration of Mr. Lincoln is destined to become historical in this respect, that the President will be freely assailed before entering office, and will be as freely applauded before he leaves it, as one who has been true to all his Constitutional duties, and false to no obligation or section.

"It may be ventured as a prediction, upon the knowledge of his past career, and of his admitted fidelity to all he believes, that Mr. Lincoln's inaugural will do more to restore harmony between the North and South, and to correct erroneous prejudices, than all the protestations of all the pretended Union Savers together. He is a Union man thouroughly, honestly and truly, and not by profession, and he will maintain every right of the South with as stern and inflexible integrity as of the North, or the East, or the West. A man born in Kentucky, bred in the vicissitudes of this giant West, who has had to carve out his own fortunes, the son and the grandson of Virginians who sprung from old Berks, in Pennsylvania, is not apt to have much other blood in his veins than what is national and American.

"Of simple tastes and habits, Mr. Lincoln lives here the calm and serene life of a respected and contented citizen, without the least pretension or affectation whatever. A genial companion, a faithful friend, and in all the domestic relations an example, he is universally esteemed as deservedly enjoying a lot which befalls but few."

BRECKINRIDGE, DOUGLAS, BELL.
THE FUSION CANDIDATES.

CHAPTER XVI.

The Fusion Candidates in New York.

A so-called "Conservative" meeting, held in Cooper Institute, September 17, 1860, was called by and composed of citizens, who, though loyal, were opposed to the election of Abraham Lincoln to the Presidency, claiming him to be a sectional candidate. The meeting was held under the auspices of the "Union Electoral Ticket" (or Anti-Lincoln) party. Every allusion made by the speakers against the election of Lincoln, was received with great applause. A few days later the committee appointed by this meeting to adopt such electoral ticket "as the crisis and the country" demanded, issued the following resolutions and the "Fusion list" of Presidential electors. It is curious enough to be given herein in full:

"Resolved, That this committee recommend to all citizens of the State of New York who are opposed to the election of Lincoln and Hamlin, and who are in favor of preserving the Union of these States upon the basis of the Constitution, the following ticket for the election of President and Vice President of the United States:

UNION ELECTORAL TICKET.

For State Electors, New York.

Herman J. Redfield, Gennessee, Douglas.
Henry S. Randall, Cortland, Breckinridge.

For District Electors:

1. Selah B. Strong, Queen, Douglas.
2. John H. Brower, Kings, Breckinridge.
3. J. A. Westervelt, New York, Breckinridge.
4. Elijah F. Purdy, New York, Douglas
5. William A. Robbe, New York, Breckinridge.
6. J. Depeyster Ogden, New York, Bell.

7. William B. Duncan, New York, Breckinridge.
8. Stephen P. Russell, New York, Breckinridge.
9. Abram B. Conger, Westchester, Breckinridge.
10. Daniel B. St. John, Orange, Bell.
11. Elisha B. Strong, Green, Douglas.
12. William Kent, Dutchess, Bell.
13. Martin Springer, Ransselaer, Douglas.
14. James Kidd, Albany, Bell.
15. Isaiah Blood, Saratoga, Douglas.
16. Henry H. Ross, Essex, Bell.
17. David C. Judson, St. Lawrence, Douglas.
18. Charles Goodyear, Schoharie, Douglas.
19. George C. Clyde, Otsego, Douglas.
20. Edward Huntington, Oneida, Bell.
21. Ambrose C. Higgins, Cortland, Douglas.
22. Lucius B. Crocker, Oswego, Douglas.
23. Pierson Mundy, Jefferson, Douglas.
24. John M. Strong, Onondaga, Douglas.
25. Edward M. Anderson, Wayne, Douglas.
26. James M. Pulver, Ontario, Bell.
27. Miles H. French, Tompkins, Bell.
28. Charles H. Carroll, Steuben, Bell.
29. Addison Gardiner, Monroe, Douglas.
30. John B. Skinner, 2d, Wyoming, Douglas.
31. Lorenzo Burrows, Orleans, Bell.
32. William Williams, Erie, Douglas.
33. Stephen D. Caldwell, Chatauqua, Douglas.

Recapitulation.

Douglas men.................................... 18
Bell and Everett men........................... 10
Breckinridge men............................... 7

                                                35

"THE VOX POPULI.

Monster Mass Meeting of Minute Men.

Tremendous Demonstration at the Cooper Institute and in the Surrounding Streets.

Ratification of the Union Electoral Ticket.

Enthusiastic Turnout of the Masses.

Over Thirty Thousand People on Duty Last Night.

The Country Safe.

Guns, Music, Banners, Torches, Sky Rockets and Songs.

Speeches of John A. Dix, James W. Gerard, Hon. John Cochrane, Charles O'Conor, General Hiram Walbridge, Judge Thompson, Theodore B. Tomlinson, James Brooks and Others.

The Union Electoral Tickets Ratified by Acclamation.

Our Country One and Inseparable.

The Fanatics and Disunionists Rebuked.

The Republicans a One-Eyed Cyclops and Hybrid Monstrosity, Etc., Etc., Etc."

—New York Herald.

CHAPTER XVII.

Old Abe Receiving the News of the Returns of His Election.

(Correspondence of the "Missouri Democrat.")
Springfield, Illinois, November 7, 1860.

There was very little sleeping done in this place last night. Everybody, by common consent, was voted a Wide-Awake, and the scenes and noises, between the closing of the polls yesterday and sunrise to-day, defy description. About 7 o'clock last evening the fun commenced. At that hour a large crowd assembled in the Assembly Chambers in the State House, prepared to hear the returns. Outside an immense crowd congregated in front of the Court House, and, when the first report came that Lincoln was seventy majority on the straight ticket, a shout went up which in a few moments was echoed all over town. Mr. Lincoln's room in the Capitol was, however, at that early hour the central point of interest. Dispatches were expected every few moments, and the crowd pressed in so fast that somebody suggested that they be requested to withdraw. This proposition instantly met with a protest from Mr. Lincoln. He said he had never done such a thing in his life, and wouldn't commence now. But the crowd pressed till the room became absolutely unbearable. Mr. Lincoln was calm and collected as ever in his life; but, when a messenger from the telegraph

STATE HOUSE (NOW COURT HOUSE),
Springfield, Illinois, 1860.

office entered, there was a nervous twitch on his countenance, that indicated an anxiety within that no coolness from without could repress. His first dispatch was from Decatur, Illinois, announcing a handsome Republican gain. It was received with shouts, and borne into the Assembly Hall as a trophy of victory to be read to the crowd. News came in slowly, but about 8 o'clock O. M. Hatch, Secretary of State, received a dispatch from Jacksonville, showing a Republican gain of 210. This dispatch seemed to gratify Mr. Lincoln exceedingly. Jacksonville was the home of Dick Yates, who had barely redeemed his promise to give a good account of himself in Morgan. Conversation followed upon the prospect in Sangamon, in which our late candidate expressed a deep interest. His attachment to Lyman Trumbull was manifested throughout the evening by various inquiries as to the Legislative ticket in this county, where our friends hoped for and have achieved a gain of two members. Probably a desire for a home indorsement added to his interest in Sangamon. The "boys" kept bringing various reports of the progress of counting, but none of them were satisfactory. About 9 o'clock Mr. Lincoln, accompanied by Auditor DuBois, Secretary Hatch and three others, left his room and proceeded, by invitation of the superintendent of the telegraph lines, Mr. Wilson, to the telegraph office. Here the returns came in more rapidly. Illinois appeared all right.

A return from Decatur, Perry County, gave great satisfaction, as Fremont received in 1856 only half the votes in the entire county that Lincoln received in a single precinct. This glimmer of light from Egypt was encouraging. It was followed by a report from Indianapolis that the Republicans of Indiana had made large gains over the October vote. Then came Alton, and it created quite a sensation. "Alton, 12 majority for Lincoln; county sure." This was the best news yet. Alton had been expected to go at least 100 for Douglas. A bad break streak was felt when a dispatch to the "State Register" announced a Democratic majority of 600 in Adams, the county in which Quincy is situated. At first it was not believed; but still there was the same authority for that as for the others, and it had to be stood. A thrill of delight was occasioned by a report that Joliet had given Douglas only 432 majority, inasmuch as 500 majority was conceded A more joyous thrill was occasioned by the news from Chicago—2,500 majority for Lincoln, and 4,000 in Cook County. "Send it to the boys," said Mr. Lincoln, and half a minute after the crowd in the State House attested its approbation by prolonged shouts of applause. Bloomington came booming in with 406 for Lincoln, and then Tolona, in Champaign County, with a large Republican gain; scattering returns from Wisconsin came along, mixed in with new dispatches, indicating Republican gains. Ten o'clock struck, and the inquiry for New York began to grow impatient. "Why don't we have something from New York?" and "I wish we could get word from New York," were the current expressions. At twenty minutes past ten a dispatch came for Lyman Trumbull, and almost simultaneously Mr.

THE POLITICAL REVOLUTION OF 1860.   137

LINCOLN RECEIVING VISITORS IN THE STATE HOUSE, SPRINGFIELD, ILL.

Trumbull came in at the door, having worked at Alton till the polls closed, and then jumped aboard the cars and reached Springfield, as stated,. Mr. Trumbull was overjoyed by the report from Madison, and continually exclaimed, "We've got 'em; we've got 'em." The Alton news was confirmed, and the jubilance at first caused was increased by the additional returns from Upper Alton and Monticello, which made Madison County and a gain of two Representatives sure. Pretty soon the operator read off a Missouri dispatch, the vote of Herman: Lincoln, 226; Douglas, 84; Bell, 13; Breckinridge, 16; and, if there was joy upon the countenance of Mr. Lincoln before, it was then a positive blaze of delight.

"You received 400 votes in St. Joseph, Missouri, Mr. Lincoln," said the operator, and positively the news seemed too good to be true. "Hannibal City, 225 votes for Lincoln." Missouri was then the theme; and, as the champion of Republicanism warmed in it, he expressed a desire to hear from St. Louis, and in an instant the question was asked, "What has Frank Blair's constituency done?" We were not long in waiting. The ticking was translated: "St. Louis County, fifteen precincts to hear from, which gave Barrett 61 majority only, give Lincoln 945 plurality over Douglas, and 9,000 over Breckinridge." "Good! good!" said everybody, in one accord. Mr. Trumbull expressed himself satisfied beyond any expectation. He had heard that Republicans were going to vote for

Bell, and was afraid that Douglas would have a plurality. Mr. Lincoln was very much pleased with this report. Further returns from Missouri were read, by which it appeared, that, in every precinct and county, the Republicans had a few votes--enough, at all events, to form the nucleus of a great party hereafter, and the point was commented upon by those in the room with satisfaction. Kansas City, with 185 for Lincoln; Cole County, with 53 for Lincoln, and other places, were read over and over again. Then, as if the slaveholding States were determined to rebuke the charges of sectionalism against Lincoln, the votes of Wheeling, with 600; Baltimore, with 1,062, and Alexandria, Virginia, with 10 Republican votes; and little Delaware, with 200 majority in Wilmington, and a gain of a Republican Congressman, swelled the glad tidings. These bits of news from Virginia, Maryland, Missouri and Delaware were duly communicated to the State House, and produced a fresh outburst of enthusiasm.

The next news was from Pittsburg, and as it was read aloud, "Alleghany County 10,000 majority for Lincoln," the surprise had a marked effect, for, in truth, it was unexpected. A dispatch from Philadelphia followed—"15,000 plurality, and 5,000 majority over all." It was hard to say which feeling was then uppermost—surprise or pleasure. Mr. Lincoln remarked that this was better than he expected—far better. It was confirmed by the following brief but pertinent dispatch from Senator Cameron:

Phil., Nov. 6, p. m.

"Hon. A. Lincoln: Pennsylvania, 70,000 for you. New York safe. Glory enough. S. CAMERON."

This was the first from New York, but was too vague to be satisfactory; and, as it was now nearly midnight, there was a brisk renewal of the impatience to hear from New York. Mr. Lincoln, Mayor ——, of Springfield, Senator Trumbell and others were invited to step across the street and partake of a collation prepared by the Republican ladies of Springfield for the entertainment of their friends. All hands accordingly repaired to the place, and found a long table well spread with eatables. The hall was pretty well crowded, and as Mr. Lincoln entered, there was of course a general commotion. The ladies rushed forward to shake hands, and it was. "How do you do, Mr. President?" from a hundred feminine voices all at the same moment The hero of the occasion went through with the required handshaking amid a chorus of singers, who struck up, meanwhile:

"We're the Lincoln boys!
We're the Lincoln boys!
Ain't you glad you joined the Republicans?
Joined the Republicans?
Ain't you glad you joined the Republicans?"

The ladies added their voices to the music of the merriest, and a more inspiring scene was seldom witnessed. The ladies were soon congratulating each other. "Oh, I've shaken hands with Lincoln," remarks one blushing fair one to another. "Have you?" replies the second; "Well, I've done better than that, for I was at the head of the table when he came in, and had a shake there, and then ran around and took my place at the foot of the line, and shook hands with him again."

While this was in progress a dispatch arrived at the telegraph office from Simeon Draper announcing that the city of New York complete gave the Fusionists only 27,600. It was carried to Mr. Lincoln, and a duplicate sent to the State House.

It is utterly impossible to describe the scene which ensued. As Mr. Lincoln read it, ladies and gentlemen closed in and overwhelmed him with congratulations. "Oh, you are elected now," said the ladies; and "It is all safe," said the gentlemen. These remarks, with variations, poured in for ten minutes; and, if Mr. Lincoln left the telegraph office for the purpose of taking a little refreshment, he came as near being killed by kindness as a man can conveniently be without serious results.

At the State House the scene was five times as bad; men pushed each other—threw up their hats, hurrahed, cheered for Lincoln, cheered for New York, cheered for everybody; and actually lay down on the carpeted floor and rolled over and over. It was some time before order could be restored to read the second dispatch from Simeon Draper:

"New York 50,000 majority for Lincoln!" And then another scene: "Did you hear that?" "Where's Douglas?" "Hit him again!" "Three cheers for the Empire State!" These are only samples of the remarks. The applause was tremendous. The Illinois State House never before heard such a noise, and probably never will again. It was beyond description; and, as New York was the culminating point of doubt, groups commenced to leave —not to go to bed—but to let the town know the result. Some went one way, and some another, yelling like demons: "New York 50,000 majority for Lincoln—whoop, whoop, hurrah!" And Springfield went off like one immense cannon report, with shouting from houses, shouting from stores, shouting from house tops and shouting everywhere. Parties ran through the streets singing, "Ain't I glad I joined the Republicans?" till they were too hoarse to speak. This news was a complete squelcher for the Douglasites. They closed their headquarters and sneaked away.

Mr. Lincoln and his friends returned to the telegraph office, and in a few minutes examined further New York returns, which confirmed the private dispatch, and made everything sure by a large majority. The press reports commenced by claiming 40,000 majority for Fusion; but step by step it receded to 38,000, 35,000, 30,000, and then to a little over 28,000. Buffalo city vote was selected as a standard upon which to calculate the effect of Fusion, and, when it was known that Lincoln had a majority of nearly 400, the case was considered settled. It was argued, that, as Fillmore and Buchanan together led Fremont several thousand in Buffalo, and Lincoln now received a majority, it was proof that the Americans would not go Fusion very generally throughout the State. This test solved all further apprehension about New York. All night there was howling for Lincoln, cheers for "Old Abe" kept up, and towards morning some of the boys procured a cannon and fired several rounds. This morning Mr. Lincoln was received at the State House by a host of friends, who have warmly congratulated him upon his election. He is emphatically a man of the people, and greeted the meanest dressed with equal cordiality as the best. This is practical Democracy—illustrated.

TO ABRAHAM LINCOLN.

Lincoln, the votes of millions of thy friends
Have placed thee at the helm, to steer this ship.
This mighty Ship of States, through calm and storm,
And, from its perilous voyage, bring it safe,
To be returned to them who gave it thee.

Dost know how fearful is the post thou holdst?
Oh! canst thou, with a steady eye and hand,
Stand firmly and swerve not, when comes the shock
Of wave quick meeting wave—for meet they must—
And thy great ship is tossed and torn as when
A leaflet passes on a summer gale?
Canst tutor well thy crew that all obey,
And suffer thee to lead; that when the storm
Shall break in fury on thy noble ship,
They'll look to thee, and see that thou art bold,
That thou art prudent, and that no rash act
Of thine shall jeopardize their precious lives?
And, when the storm is past, and calm, once more,
Shall mirror sunshine and cerulean skies,
Oh! may they say: "Most noble man, to thee
Is due all praise; the storm is o'er, and now
Our ship is safe, the sun shines brightly down,
And everything betokens peace and joy."

Result of the Presidential Election of November 6, 1860.

STATES.	Electoral Vote.				Popular Vote.			
	Lincoln.	Bell.	Douglas.	Breckinridge.	Lincoln.	Bell.	Douglas.	Breckinridge.
Maine	8				62,811	2,046	26,693	6,368
New Hampshire	5				37,519	441	25,881	2,112
Massachusetts	13				106,533	22,331	34,372	5,939
Rhode Island	4				12,244		*7,707	
Connecticut	6				43,792	3,291	15,522	14,641
Vermont	5				33,808	1,969	6,849	218
New York	35				362,646		*312,510	
New Jersey	4		3		58,324		*62,801	
Pennsylvania	27				268,030	12,776	16,765	*178,871
Delaware				3	8,815	3,864	1,023	7,337
Maryland				8	2,294	41,760	5,966	42,482
Virginia		15			1,929	74,681	16,290	74,323
North Carolina				10		44,990	2,701	48,539
South Carolina				8	No	popular	vote	
Georgia				10		42,886	11,590	51,889
Kentucky		12			1,364	66,058	25,651	53,143
Tennessee		12				69,274	11,350	64,709
Ohio	23				231,610	12,194	187,232	11,405
Louisiana				6		20,204	7,625	22,681
Mississippi				7		25,040	3,283	40,797
Indiana	13				139,033	5,306	115,509	12,295
Illinois	11				172,161	4,913	160,215	2,404
Alabama				9		27,875	13,651	48,831
Missouri			9		17,028	58,372	58,801	31,317
Arkansas				4		20,094	5,227	28,732
Michigan	6				88,480		405	65,057	805
Florida				3		5,437	367	8,543
Texas				4		*15,438		47,548
Iowa	4				70,409	1,763	55,111	1,048
Wisconsin	5				86,110	161	65,021	888
California	4				39,173	6,817	38,516	34,334
Minnesota	4				22,069	62	11,920	748
Oregon	3				5,270	183	3,951	5,006
Totals	180	39	12	72	1,866,452	590,631	1,375,157	847,953

Lincoln over Douglas	491,295
Lincoln over Breckinridge	1,018,499
Lincoln over Bell	1,275,821
Other Candidates over Lincoln	947,289

* Fusion.

CHAPTER XVIII.

Charles Sumner's Great Speech on the Election of Lincoln.

(From the "Boston Journal," November 9, 1865.)

Charles Sumner lectured in Concord, Massachusetts, yesterday evening, on the "Life, Character and Public Services of General Lafayette." After the lecture, the Concord Wide-Awakes, deeming this a fitting time to call upon our Senator, formed, and with a drum corps marched to the residence of Mr. Ralph Waldo Emerson; and, after cheers had been given for Hon. Charles Sumner, he appeared, and was addressed by Hon. J. S. Keyes, in behalf of the Wide-Awakes. Mr. Sumner replied:

"Captain and Wide-Awakes: You take me entirely by surprise. I came here to-night to perform an agreeable service, not of a political character. I had not anticipated any such opportunity as this with which you now honor me. Nor did I anticipate any such welcome. Let me thank you most sincerely for the kind and good words that have come from your Captain. They are to me a reward for what little service I may have been able to render in the past. They will encourage me to what I hope to do in the future. I join with you in gladness at what has occurred, at the victory which we are now celebrating. Victories are sometimes won by the cartridge box, sometimes by the ballot box; but I doubt whether any victory won by the cartridge box involves higher principles or more important results than that which has now been won by the ballot box. A poet has said that the shot fired here was heard round the world; and I doubt not that this victory which we have achieved in our country will cause a reverberation that will be heard throughout the civilized globe. People, everywhere, who are struggling for rights, who are vindicating liberal ideas, who are seeking human improvement, will be encouraged when they hear of yesterday. It will be good news to Garabaldi, in Italy; it will be good news to the French, who are now suffering under despotic power; and it will be, my friends, good news to all of us, for it tells a great change has occurred.

"Every four years we choose a new President, but it very rarely happens that we choose a new government. But yesterday we not only chose a new President, but a new Government. A new order of things was inaugurated by the vote of yesterday, which will put our country under a new direction, and lift it up to the platform of principles on which it was originally placed by our forefathers. Several things may be considered to be fairly established by the vote of yesterday, if we look at it in a practical light. First, the American people have declared, according to the very words of Madison, that it was wrong to admit into the Constitution the idea that there can be property in men. They have declared that slavery, if it exists anywhere, is sectional, and must derive all such life as it has from local laws, not from the Constitution; in other words, that slavery is sectional, and freedom national; in opposition to the idea which has been put forward so often, that freedom was sectional, and slavery national. In the second place, the American people have declared, by this vote, that all the outlying Territories of the Government, so enormous in extent, and destined to be inhabited by an immense population, shall be consecrated to freedom; that the soil shall never be pressed by the footstep of a slave. In the third place, they have declared that the old original policy of the fathers of the administration of the National Government shall be adopted, in opposition to the slave policy which has been especially pursued for the last twelve years, and more or less during the last forty years. They have declared that the slave trade, which it is now proposed to open with increased activity, shall be in reality suppressed, and that all the power of the Government shall be directed in that direction. These things have been declared by that vote solemnly and in a way from which there can be no appeal. Surely this is a great action for our country, and forms a landmark in its history. Having obtained this great victory, it now remains that we should know how to use it with moderation, with prudence, with wisdom. I believe that Abraham Lincoln has those elements of character that will enable him to carry us through this crisis; that he is prudent, wise, discreet, and also brave. I believe that bravery is necessary in directing the affairs of government, as much as prudence. I believe he is the man especially called to see to it that we are not in any way checked or set back by the menaces of disunion which sometimes come to us from the South, and are repeated in Massachusetts. To these menaces we deem it necessary to make no other reply than to proceed with our work in the spirit of the Constitution, wisely, prudently, answering their threats with 'The Union shall be preserved,' and it will be more precious by its consecration to human freedom."

CHAPTER XIX.

Campaign Songs.

HONEST ABE OF THE WEST.

Air—"Star Spangled Banner."

O, hark! from the pine-crested hills of old Maine,
　Where the splendor first falls from the wings of the morning,
And away in the West, over river and plain,
　Rings out the grand anthem of Liberty's warning!
　　From green-rolling prairie it swells to the sea,
　　For the people have risen, victorious and free
　　They have chosen their leaders, and bravest and best
　　Of them all is Old Abe, Honest Abe of the West!

The spirit that fought for the patriots of old
　Has swept through the land and aroused us forever;
In the pure air of heaven a standard unfold
　Fit to marshal us on to the sacred endeavor!
　　Proudly the banner of freemen we bear;
　　Noble the hopes that encircle it there!
　　And where battle is thickest we follow the crest
　　Of gallant Old Abe, Honest Abe of the West!

There's a triumph in urging a glorious cause,
　Though the hosts of the foe for a while may be stronger,
Pushing on for just rules and holier laws,
　Till their lessening columns oppose us no longer.

THE POLITICAL REVOLUTION OF 1860.

But ours the loud paean of men who have past
Through the struggles of years, and are victors at last;
So forward the flag! leave to Heaven the rest,
And trust in Old Abe, Honest Abe of the West!

Lo! see the bright scroll of the Future unfold!
Broad farms and fair cities shall crown our devotion—
Free Labor turn even the sand into gold,
And the links of her railway chain ocean to ocean;
Barks that float on the dark river waves
With a wealth never wrung from the sinews of slaves;
And the Chief, in whose rule all the land shall be blest,
Is our noble Old Abe, Honest Abe of the West!

Then on to the holy Republican strife!
And again, for a future as fair as the morning,
For the sake of that freedom more precious than life,
Ring out the grand anthem of Liberty's warning!
Lift the banner on high, while from mountain and plain,
The cheers of the people are sounded again;
Hurrah! for our cause—of all causes the best!
Hurrah! for Old Abe, Honest Abe of the West!
—Edmund C. Stedman.

OLD ABE'S PRELIMINARY VISIT TO THE WHITE HOUSE.

Air—"Villikins and his Dinah."

One Abr'am there was who lived out in the West,
Esteemed by his neighbors the wisest and best;
And you'll see, on a time, if you follow my ditty,
How he took a straight walk up to Washington city.
Ri tu, etc.

His home was in Springfield, out in Illinois,

Where he'd long been the pride of the men and "the boys,"
But he left the white house with no sign of regret,
For he knew that the people had another to let.
   Ri tu, etc.

So Abr'am he trudged on to Washington straight,
And reached the White House through the Avenue gate,
Old Buck and his cronies (some chaps from the South)
Sat round the East room rather down in the mouth.
   Ri tu, etc.

Old Abe seized the knocker and gave such a thump,
Buck thought the state ship had run into a stump;
He trembled all over and turned deadly pale,
"That noise," said he, "must have been made with a rail."
   Ri tu, etc.

"Run, Lewis, run, Jerry, and open the door"—
And the "functionary" nearly fell down on the floor—
"There's only one man that knocks that way, I'm blessed!
And he is that tarnal old Abe of the West."
   Ri tu, etc.

The Cabinet, frightened, sat still in their seats,
While Abr'am impatient the rapping repeats;
"I hope it ain't Abe," said old Buck, pale and gray.
"If it is, boys, there'll be here the devil to pay."
   Ri tu, etc.

'At last, tho' reluctant, Buck opened the door,
And found a chap waiting, six feet three or four;
"I've come, my fine fellows," said Abe to the ring,
"To give you fair notice to vacate next spring."
   Ri tu, etc.

"The people have watched you, and made up their mind
That your management's running the country behind;

You're badly in debt, and your plan is a bold one—
To make a new debt to pay off the old one.
   Ri tu, etc.

"You and Douglas have so split your party in twain
That Spaulding's best glue can't unite it again;
And both parts are useless, the Country don't need 'em—
For one goes for Slavery and the other 'gainst Freedom.
   Ri tu, etc.

LINCOLN AND LIBERTY.

Hail to the chief who in power advances!
 Shout for the cause that has tarried so long!
Sing! for the glory of mercy enhances,
 And spent is the spell of the fetter and thong!
   Hail to the gallant crest
   Gleaming above the West!
Hail to the lofty, the blameless and true!
   Hark to the people's cry—
   Lincoln and Liberty!
Lincoln shall triumph and Liberty too!

Thunder the tocsin! Ho, leap at the warning
 Into the lists of a leader so true!
And on the light of a heavenly morning,
 The martyrs of Liberty languished to view!
   Hail to the gallant crest, etc.

Strike, freemen, strike for the pride of the nation!
 Strain every nerve for the hope of the Free!
And, O, soon the dawn of a day of salvation
 To millions unborn shall meridian see!
   Hail to the gallant crest
   Gleaming above the West!
Hail to the lofty, the blameless, and true!
   Hark to the people's cry—
   Lincoln and Liberty!
Lincoln shall triumph and Liberty too!

OLD ABE, THE RAIL SPLITTER.

Tune—"The Star Spangled Banner."

Hark! hear ye the shouts which are shaking the hills,
   And filling with gladness our country's green valleys!
'Tis the name of "Old Abe" that has magic which thrills
   The hearts of the legions whom Freedom now rallies.
O, that name has a charm, like the tocsin's alarm,
Which causes the freeman for conflict to arm;
No more will they bow, like a bevy of slaves,
To the dotards who rule as the tools of the knaves.

Too long has our country been cursed by the sway
   Of men who are living to multiply evil;
It is time to arouse, and to despots cry, Nay.
   The spreading of slavery—work of the devil—
At a Democrat's hand may seem ever so grand,
But cannot proceed in this rail-splitting land;
For "Honest Old Abe," uneclipsed at his trade,
Is mauling the rails and the fence will be made.

We freemen have chosen this hard-working man—
   The friend of free-labor and honest requital—
To summon us toilers, and keeping the van,
   To finish the work to Humanity vital.
No more soil which the brave, who are now in the grave,
Shed their blood from the grasp of Oppression to save,
Must be turned into "commons" for men of black skin;
So the rails of "Old Abe" will the darkies fence in!

                       —Jesse Clement.
Dubuque, Iowa, May 24, 1860.

HURRAH FOR LINCOLN.

Tune—"Boatman's Dance."

Hurrah! hurrah! did you hear the news!
The Democrats have got the blues;

THE POLITICAL REVOLUTION OF 1860.

They're puzzled now, and all afraid,
Because we've nominated Abe.
  Then, shout, freemen, shout!
  Shout, freemen, shout!
    We'll all unite,
    And bravely fight
  For the Star of Freedom's dawning.
    Hi! ho! we'll put them through,
    Split their rails and haul them too;
    Hi! ho! we'll put them through,
    Split their rails and haul them too!

In all their ranks they cannot find
A candidate to suit their mind;
They kick and squirm, but 'tis no use,
Their game is up, their platform's loose.
  Then shout, freemen, shout!
  Shout, freemen, shout!
    We'll all unite,
    And bravely fight
  For the Star of Freedom's dawning.
    Hi! ho! etc.

They know that they will lose the day
If they take up Stephen A.;
And so to add to their humbug swell,
I think they'd better take up Bell.
  Then shout, freemen, shout!
  Shout, freemen, shout!
    We'll all unite,
    And bravely fight
  For the Star of Freedom's dawning.
    Hi! ho! etc.

I hear they've bought an old steamtug
On which to place poor Little Dug;
For President too late they've found

His coat tail comes too near the ground.
  Then shout, freemen, shout!
  Shout, freemen, shout!
    We'll all unite,
    And bravely fight
  For the Star of Freedom's dawning.
    Hi! ho! etc.

We'll give them Ham enough this fall
To satisfy them one and all,
Served up in style quite neat and plain,
Just imported from Old Maine.
  Then shout, freemen, shout!
  Shout, freemen, shout!
    We'll all unite,
    And bravely fight
  For the Star of Freedom's dawning.
    Hi! ho! etc.

Hurrah! hurrah! we are sure to win,
And the way we'll beat will be a sin;
The coming year's impending blast
Will show that they have crowed their last.
  Then shout, freemen, shout!
  Shout, freemen, shout!
    We'll all unite,
    And bravely fight
  For the Star of Freedom's dawning.
    Hi! ho! we'll put them through,
    Split their rails and haul them too,
    Hi! ho! we'll put them through,
    Split their rails and haul them too,

WE'LL VOTE FOR LINCOLN.

    Air—"Wait for the Wagon."
Come, all ye friends of freedom

In every noble State,
  Come vote for Abra'm Lincoln,
    Our worthy candidate.
A statesman true and honest,
  He's proved himself at home,
But now we'll send him from us
  For four long years to come.

CHORUS.

We'll all vote for Lincoln,
We'll all vote for Lincoln,
We'll all vote for Lincoln,
  Our country's steadfast friend.

The man whom we have chosen
  Is one of humble birth;
We love him for his virtues—
  His purity and worth.
We know he's firm and faithful,
  Undaunted and sincere,
And friends of truth and justice
  His honored name revere.

We'll all vote for Lincoln,
We'll all vote for Lincoln,
We'll all vote for Lincoln,
  Our country's faithful friend.

We'll trust the bark of freedom
  To Lincoln's watchful care;
He'll pilot us in safety
  Through every hidden snare;
We'll fear no furious breakers
  While he is at the helm—
No waves of strife or discord
  Our bark can overwhelm.

We'll all vote for Lincoln,
We'll all vote for Lincoln,
We'll all vote for Lincoln,
The Union's truest friend.

Of this, our great Republic,
  He'll prove a noble son,
And in his country's service,
  Another Washington.
So till the contest's ended
  His praises we will sing,
And then with shouts of triumph
  We'll make the welkin ring.

We'll then shout for Lincoln,
We'll then shout for Lincoln,
We'll then shout for Lincoln,
OUR HONEST PRESIDENT!
—Linda Lindon.

COME AND VOTE WITH ME.

Of all the men for President,
  In the East or in the West,
We think that honest Abraham
  Is the greatest and the best.
    O will you, won't you, don't you
    Want to come and vote with me?

Some talk of running Douglas,
  Some talk of running Bell;
But we think that honest Abraham
  Will suit us just as well.
    O will you, won't you, etc.

Come, all you landless freemen

LINCOLN MEDALS OF 1860.

That want good land to till,
Elect old honest Abraham,
And get the Homestead Bill.
    O will you, won't you, etc.

Then you can have a pleasant home
Away in the far West,
Where the land and the water
Is of the very best.
    O will you, won't you, etc.

We have tried him as a soldier,
We know that he will fight;
We have tried him as a statesman,
And know that he is right.
    O will you, won't you, etc.

We have tried him as a farmer,
We know he is no shirk,
And when he followed splitting rails
He was not afraid of work.
    O will you, won't you, etc.

We have tried him as a lawyer,
And know that he is true;
And none so well for President
As Honest Abe, will do.
    O will you, won't you, etc.

The sixth of next November
His opponents will see,
They are so much like Crockett's dog,
They bark up the wrong tree.
    O will you, won't you, etc.

If you wish an honest President
For four successive years,

Come with your hearts and voices,
And give old Abe three cheers.
O will you, won't you, etc.

POOR LITTLE DUG.

(A New Nigger Song to an Old Nigger Tune.)
Dere was a little man, and his name was Stevy Dug,
To de White House he longed for to go;
But he hadn't any votes through de whole of de Souf,
In de place where votes ought to grow.

CHORUS.
So it ain't no use for to blow—
Dat little game of brag won't go;
He can't get de vote, 'case de tail ob his coat
Is hung just a little too low.

His legs dey was short, but his speeches dey was long,
And nuffin but hisself could he see;
His principles was weak, but his spirits dey was strong,
For a thirsty little soul was he.
CHORUS—So it ain't no use for to blow, etc.

He couldn't sleep nights for de nigger in de fence,
So his health it began for to fail;
And he suffered berry much from de 'fects of a ride
Dat he got on a Lincoln rail.
CHORUS—So it ain't no use for to blow, etc.

He shivered and he shook in de cold North blast,
And de wind from de Souf dat blew;
But de Locofoco ship hove him overboard at last,
So his friends had to all heave-to.

CHORUS.
So it ain't no use for to blow—

Dat little game of brag won't go;
He can't get de vote, 'case de tail ob his coat
Is hung just a little too low.

LINCOLN AND HAMLIN—GOD BLESS THEM!

Air—"Columbia the Gem of the Ocean."

There's a sound like the surges of ocean,
  Or winds sweeping forest and lea;
It comes from a nation in motion—
  From the millions who've sworn to be free!
There are thoughts, beyond words, which impress them,
  As they shout with enraptured applause—
"Here's to Lincoln and Hamlin! God bless them!
  And bless, too, our country and cause!"

CHORUS.

And bless, too, our country and cause!
And bless, too, our country and cause!
Here's to Lincoln and Hamlin! God bless them!
And bless, too, our country and cause!

Through the portals of death speak the sires,
  Aroused from their haven of rest,
To kindle the slumbering fires,
  Till they glow in each patriot's breast!
They stretch out their arms to caress them—
  Their children, who honor their laws—
And cry—"Lincoln and Hamlin, God bless them!
  And bless, too, our country and cause!"

CHORUS.

And bless, too, our country and cause, etc.

The future speaks out with its voices,
   And joins with the rest of all time,
As it smiles with delight, and rejoices
   At a scene more than grand—that's sublime!
And vain is the hope to suppress them,
   Or to stifle the shouts of applause
Which cry—"Lincoln and Hamlin, God bless them!
   And bless, too, our country and cause!"

CHORUS.

And bless, too, our country and cause, etc.

LINCOLN SONG.

Tune—"Highland Laddie."

Oh where, tell me where, was this Abra'm Lincoln born?
Oh where, tell me where, was this Abra'm Lincoln born?
In a cabin down in old Kentuck, one cheerless wintry morn,
And on Hardin county hills he was trained to plowing corn.
    In a cabin, etc.

Oh what, tell me what, means this sound that fills the air?
Oh what, tell me what, means this sound that fills the air?
It is the welcome voice that comes from freemen everywhere,
Shouting "Hail to Abe Lincoln, the plowman's son and heir!"
    It is the welcome, etc.

Oh why, tell me why, do the loud huzzas begin?
Oh why, tell me why, do the loud huzzas begin?
It is because at mauling rails "Abe's" practiced hand is "in,"
And the people know in Freedom's fight his mauling hand will
    win.
    It is because, etc.

Oh, who leads the yeomen in battle, tell me who?
Oh, who leads the yeomen in battle, tell me who?
It is "Old Honest Abe," my boys, who stands some six-feet-
    two—
And a noble, stalwart warrior, to freedom ever true.
    It is "Old Honest Abe," etc.

By whom, tell me whom, will November's fight be won?
By whom, tell me whom, will November's fight be won?
The Democratic spoilsmen horde will soon begin to run,
And our rail-mauling candidate will march to Washington,
    The Democratic, etc.

Oh what, tell me what, then will virtuous Jemmy do?
Oh what, tell me what, then will virtuous Jemmy do?
He'll "follow in the footsteps" of his office-holding crew,
And with Fowler, down in Cuba, strike for slavery anew.
    He'll follow, etc.

                              Llew. Curry.

THE RAIL SPLITTERS.

Tune—"Uncle Ned."

We've a noble rail splitter, and his name is Honest Abe,
    And he lives in Illinois, as you know;
And he has all the tools there to carry on his trade,
    And the way he piles them up isn't slow.

CHORUS.

    So lay down your Democratic hoe-o-o,
    And hang up your Democratic bow-o-o;
    There's no more hard work for poor old Jim,
    Kase he's gone where the Locofocos go.

But the people said to Abe, lay your rail splitting by,
    For we want to try your muscles on the course;
Here's a Locofoco Giant forty-seven inches high,
    Who imagines he can travel like a horse.
        CHORUS—So lay down your Democratic hoe-o-o, etc.

THE POLITICAL REVOLUTION OF 1860.

But we think the chances slim for this little Giant Doug,
    For the rail splitter runs like a hound;
Then he has to paddle through all the Democratic mud,
    With his coat-tail so close to the ground.
        CHORUS—So lay down your Democratic hoe-o-o, etc.

Then there is Breck from Old Kentucky, who is right on the track
    Where the Little Giant wants to pass along,
And he says he will never carry Stephen on his back,
    For he don't feel himself very strong.
        CHORUS—So lay down your Democratic hoe-o-o, etc.

So they had it up and down while the rail splitter run,
    Till the White House appeared in his view;
Then said old Buck to Abe, why the nation did you come?
    Why, said Abe, I had nothing else to do.
        CHORUS—So lay-down your Democratic hoe-o-o, etc.

LINCOLN IS THE MAN.

The West is bound to have the next President,
Have the next President, have the next President,
The West is bound to have the next President,
    And Lincoln is the man.

    Yes, Lincoln is the man—yes, Lincoln is the man,
    Yes, Lincoln is the man to send to Washington.
      Ain't we glad we joined the Republicans,
        Joined the Republicans, joined the Republicans,
      Ain't we glad we joined the Republicans,
        Down in Illinois?

The Democrats have got a Little Giant,
Have got a Little Giant, have got a Little Giant,
The Democrats have got a Little Giant,
    They call him Stephen A.;
      But Lincoln is the man, etc.

A fig for their giant, for we've got a bigger one,
We've got a bigger one, we've got a bigger one,
A fig for their giant, for we've got a bigger one,
  And he is an honest man;
  But Lincoln is the man, etc.

Great big nigger come out of the wood-pile,
Out of the wood-pile, out of the wood-pile,
Great big nigger come out of the wood-pile,
  And spilled Steve's bowl of milk;
  But Lincoln is the man, etc.

The fire-eaters swear they'll blow up the Union,
Blow up the Union, blow up the Union,
The fire-eaters swear they'll blow up the Union,
  If we dare to spill their milk;
  Oh, Lincoln is the man, etc.

But we'll string them up on a flat-boat cable,
But we'll string them up on a flat-boat cable,
On a flat-boat cable, on a flat-boat cable,
  Just fifty cubits high.
Yes, we'll elect Old Abe, the gallant and the true,
The Union, too, we'll save, and traitors "we'll subdue."
  Oh, ain't we glad, etc.
       —Greenhorn.

WHERE, OH, WHERE!

Tune—"Where, oh! where are the Hebrew Children?"
Where, oh! where is the lordly party?
Where, oh! where is the lordly party?
Which so long has ruled the nation,
Worse and worse from year to year?

CHORUS.

Torn asunder by fierce dissensions,

Torn asunder by fierce dissensions,
Torn asunder by fierce dissensions,
Leaders all—"gone to the grass."

Where, oh! where is the valiant Stephen?
Where, oh! where is the valiant Stephen?
He who fights the Administration,
Reckless now of victory?

CHORUS.

He "went up" in the row at Charleston,
He "went up" in the row at Charleston,
He "went up" in the row at Charleston,
Chosen there to stay at home.

Where, oh! where is "Jimmy" Buchanan?
Where, oh! where is "Jimmy" Buchanan?
Who went up to the Fed'ral Mansion,
Placed there as the people's choice?

CHORUS.

He has lost all popular favor,
He has lost all popular favor,
He has lost all popular favor,
Soon he'll go from whence he came.

Here, oh! here are the people's champions;
Here, oh! here are the people's champions;
Leaders bold of the opposition,
In the fall to sweep the land.

CHORUS.

Honest Abe and Hannibal Hamlin,
Honest Abe and Hannibal Hamlin,
Honest Abe and Hannibal Hamlin,
Theirs the lead, we follow on.

Illinois to Maine sends greeting,
Illinois to Maine sends greeting,
Maine returns the salutation,
East and West the welkin rings.

CHORUS.

Three loud cheers for the people's ticket,
Three loud cheers for the people's ticket,
Three loud cheers for the people's ticket,
Hurrah! hurrah! hip, hip, hurrah!

A FINE OLD GENTLEMAN.

Tune—"The Fine Old English Gentleman."

We have a man in Illinois, a statesman true and tried,
In whom the people of the land most earnestly confide;
He is made from timber of the real genuine stuff,
The grain is good—sound at heart—and known to be quite tough.
    He's a fine old trusty gentleman,
    One of the olden kind.

He was born in old Kentucky, the home of Henry Clay;
From there he moved to the Sucker State at quite an early day,
Where he found vast prairies, with the richest kind of soil,
And for an honest living he was not afraid to toil;
    He's a fine old working gentleman,
    One of the people's kind.

He has the spirit of a man—who in this world ne'er fails;
Once a jolly boatman, then a splitter of good rails,
Whatever work he did, was sure to be well done,
And in every occupation he is always full of fun;
    He's a fine old jovial gentleman,
    As e'er you'd wish to find.

THE POLITICAL REVOLUTION OF 1860.

A good farmer, a good lawyer, and always a good neighbor,
A living representative of the dignity of labor,
By industry and study, has become a statesman learned;
His present high position he most honorably has earned.
       He's a fine old honest gentleman,
       With talents rare combined.

In fifty-eight, by the popular will, the Senatorship he won,
Although the Democratic giant then against him run.
T'was by unjust apportionment that Douglas was elected,
By his boasted popular sovereignty—he surely was rejected.
       For our own old favorite gentleman
       The people were inclined.

And now this little giant is almost in despair,
For his Democratic brethren his company can spare;
His humbug "squatter sovereignty" has squatted him clear under,
'Twas by the "nigger question" the party burst asunder.
       But our fine old winning gentleman
       Will leave them all behind.

Lincoln's not a handsome man, but certain he is tall,
And will be elected President undoubtedly this fall;
We will send him to the "White House" when "Old Buck's" time is out,
For the Democratic party will be put to utter rout
       By our fine old earnest gentleman,
       Who suits the public mind.

Unfurl the banners to the breeze, and let them proudly wave,
While Douglas men and Democrats grow mad and fiercely rave.
Our colors from the Capitol will soon be gayly floating,
While up Salt River, far away, the Locos will be boating,
       Sent by our generous gentleman,
       Cool comfort there to find.

GIVE US ABE AND HAMLIN, TOO.

Air—"A Wet Sheet and a Flowing Sea."

O, hear ye not the wild huzzas
  That come from every state,
For honest Uncle Abraham,
  The people's candidate?
He is our choice, our nominee,
  A self-made man and true;
We'll show the Democrats this fall
  What honest Abe can do.

CHORUS.

Then give us Abe and Hamlin too,
  To guide our gallant ship;
With stalwart boys to man the decks,
  We'll have a merry trip.

Come, granny Buck, you'd better go
  While you can see the way,
For I fear your nerves won't stand the shock
  On next election day.
So take your hat!—What's that you say?
  You are so cold you shiver?
Why, that's the way you'll feel, my dear,
  When sailing up Salt River.

CHORUS.

Then give us Abe and Hamlin too,
  To guide our gallant ship;
With stalwart boys to man the decks,
  We'll have a merry trip.

I hear that Dug is half inclined
  To give us all leg-bail,
Preferring exercise on foot

THE POLITICAL REVOLUTION OF 1860.

To riding on a rail;
For Abe has one already mauled
  Upon the White House plan;
If once Dug gets astride of that,
  He is a used up man.

CHORUS.

Then give us Abe and Hamlin too,
  To guide our gallant ship;
With stalwart boys to man the decks,
  We'll have a merry trip.

Come rally with us here to-night,
  Be "Wide-Awake" for fun,
For we shall surely win the day
  Before old sixty-one.
From North to South, from East to West,
  Our power shall be felt.
I tell you fight with all your might,
  For Abe shall have the belt.

CHORUS.

Then give us Abe and Hamlin too,
  To guide our gallant ship;
We'll make the Locos walk the plank,
  We'll have a merry trip.

—Mrs. L. L. Deming.

WE'RE BOUND TO WORK.

Tune—"Camptown Races."

There's an old plow "hoss" whose name is "Dug,"
  Du da, du da;
He's short and thick—a regular "plug,"
  Du da, du da day.

CHORUS.
We're bound to work all night,
We're bound to work all day;
I'll bet my money on the "Lincoln hoss;"
Who bets on Stephen A?

The "little plug" has had his day,
    Du da, du da;
He's out of the ring by all fair play,
    Du da, du da day.
        We're bound, etc.

He tried his best on the Charleston track,
    Du da, du da;
But couldn't make time with his "Squatter Jack,"
    Du da, du da day.
        We're bound, etc.

"Old Abraham's" a well bred nag,
    Du da, du da;
His wind is sound—he'll never lag,
    Du da, du da day.

In '58 he tried his gait,
    Du da, du da;
He trotted Douglas through the State,
    Du da, du da day.

In '60 now we're going to trot,
So "plank" your money on the spot,
    Du da, du da day.

The "Lincoln hoss" will never fail,
    Du da, du da;
He will not shy at ditch or "rail,"
    Du da, du da day.

The "Little Dug" can never win,
    Du da, du da;
That Kansas job's too much for him,
    Du da, du da day.

LINCOLN MEDALS OF 1860.

His legs are weak, his mind unsound,
　　Du da, du da;
His "switch tail" is too near the ground,
　　Du da, du da day.
　　　We're bound, etc.

(The Springfield Glee Club sang the above song at a ratification meeting, Springfield, Ill., June 7, 1860.)

THE RISING TIDE.

Sung at the great Republican gathering at Erie, Pa., September, 12, 1860.

They come, they come, a mighty throng,
From mountain and valley, with joyous song;
They sing of the fathers who made us free,
Of Lincoln and Hamlin and Liberty.

They come, they come, a victorious throng,
Defeating the foes we have fought so long;
As waves of the ocean subdue the sand,
They deluge the enemies of the land.

They come, they come, with armer bright,
The fearless defenders of truth and right;
No deeds of corruption their hands shall stain
While keeping unsullied our fair domain.

They come, they come, with freedom's light,
Dispelling the darkness of slavery's night,
That fain would o'ershadow our virgin soil.
Degrading forever the white man's toil.

And still they come in proud array—
O what is an age to this glorious day?
Humanity's cause let us all proclaim,
And give to the nation undying fame.

LINCOLN BANNER SONG.

Air—"From Greenland's Icy Mountains."

Who feeleth not a rapture,
  Who boundeth not in pride,
With Lincoln's banner o'er him,
  And Freedom on his side?
For him we seek no triumph,
  By whom we strive and stand,
But Liberty and Freedom,
  The glory of the land.

The bold and gallant Lincoln
  Has worn a golden name,
And now his country'll give him,
  The pinnacle of fame.
He sought the post of danger
  'Mid spirits bold and free;
And now the gallant Lincoln
  Our President shall be.

Our watchword now is Freedom,
  Our panoply and might;
We prize the people's liberty,
  Their every chartered right.
To the breeze we'll throw our banner,
  And all the world shall see,
We'll crown the gallant Lincoln
  The leader of the free.

OLD ABE AND HIS FIGHTS.

Air—"Sir Roger de Coverly."

Tell us of his fights with Douglas—
  How his spirit never quails;
Tell of us of his manly bearing,
  Of his skill in splitting rails.

Tell us he's a second Webster;
  Or, if better, Henry Clay;
That he's full of genial humor,
  Placid as a summer day.

Call him Abe, or call him Abram—
  Abraham—'tis all the same;
Abe will smell as sweet as either;
  We don't care about the name.

Say he's capable and honest,
  Loves country's good alone;
Never drank a drop of whisky,
  Wouldn't know it from a stone.

Tell us he resembles Jackson,
  Save he wears a larger boot,
And is broader 'cross the shoulders,
  And is taller by a foot.

CAMPAIGN SONG.

Tune—"Hurrah, Hurrah, Hurrah!"

Old Abe's the man to win the fight,
  Hurrah, hurrah, hurrah!
He strikes for freedom and the right,
  Hurrah, hurrah, hurrah!
He'll give old Buck his walking papers,
And make poor Dug cut wondrous capers,
  Hurrah, hurrah, hurrah!
  Hurrah, hurrah, hurrah!

The hour has brought the people's man,
  Hurrah, hurrah, hurrah!
His stalwart form shall lead the van,
  Hurrah, hurrah, hurrah!
'And freedom's battle is begun,
We will not rest till victory's won,

Our leader's true, and tried, and brave,
  Hurrah, hurrah, hurrah!
His honor will our country save,
  Hurrah, hurrah, hurrah!
And lo! he comes, his towering form
Stands firm before the rising storm.
  Hurrah, hurrah, hurrah!

Shamocracy is not the stuff,
  Hurrah, hurrah, hurrah!
Of this vile trash we've had enough;
  Hurrah, hurrah, hurrah!
Old Abe will cleanse the Augean stable,
He's ready, willing, true and able!
  Hurrah, hurrah, hurrah!

Old fossil Buck his things must pack,
  Hurrah, hurrah, hurrah!
We've got a live man on his track,
  Hurrah, hurrah, hurrah!
And Buck and Dug shall go together,
And row their craft way up Salt river,
  Hurrah, hurrah, hurrah!

LINCOLN AND LIBERTY.

By F. A. B. Simpkins.

("Honest Abe Lincoln" born in Kentucky, followed the plow and path of rectitude in Indiana, and mauled rails and Stephen A. Douglas in Illinois.)

Air—"Rosin the Bow."

Hurrah for the choice of the nation!
  Our chieftain so brave and so true;
We'll go for the great Reformation,
  For Lincoln and Liberty too!

We'll go for the son of Kentucky,
    The hero of Hoosierdom through,
The pride of the suckers so lucky,
    For Lincoln and Liberty too!

Our David's good sling is unerring,
    For slaveocrats' giant he slew;
Then shout for the Freedom preferring,
    For Lincoln and Liberty too!

They'll find what, by feeling and mauling,
    Our rail-maker statesman can do;
For the people are everywhere calling
    For Lincoln and Liberty too!

Then up with our banner so glorious,
    The Star Spangled red, white and blue;
We'll fight till our flag is victorious,
    For Lincoln and Liberty too!

"GOD AND THE RIGHT."

Hark! hark! over mountain, through forest and vale,
Borne along on the wings of the swift rushing gale,
Comes the loud battle cry of men in their might,
The watchword of freedom—"God and the right!"
    Raise your banners high,
    Shout forth the battle cry,
"Lincoln and Hamlin—God and the right!"

From Atlantic's blue waves to the far peaceful ocean
The gathering hosts of the free are in motion,
Marching steadily onward to join in the fight—
The glorious contest for "God and the right!"
    Proudly their pennants fly,
    Loud rings their battle cry,
"Lincoln and Hamlin—God and the right!"

From the field and workshop the brave sons of toil,
With one common object—Free men and Free soil—
With firm, steady hand, and with eye beaming bright,
Press onward to battle for God and the right!
    Onward the victory,
    List to their battle cry,
"Lincoln and Hamlin—God and the right!"

Hark! through the night the long tocsin is sounding,
With bright, joyous hope each bosom is bounding;
Soon on us will dawn the millennial light,
The glorious reign of God and the right!
    Shout then for Liberty,
    Join in the battle cry,
"Lincoln and Hamlin—God and the right!"

ABE LINCOLN'S EXCELSIOR.

The shades of night were falling fast
As through a Western village passed
A man who on his shoulders bore
A RAIL, in length six feet or more,
    Abe Lincoln.

Along the crowded streets he walked
While men and women loudly talked;
Old fogies turned first red, then pale,
As to and fro he swung that Rail,
    Abe Lincoln.

With rapid strides he neared the spot
By friends of Douglas not forgot,
When years ago the Giant tried
To swallow Kansas, gulped—and died—
    Abe Lincoln.

Upon the court house steps he sat
To rest his limbs, perhaps to chat,

And from his pocket brought the tale
And history of that ancient Rail,
    Abe Lincoln.

That history we may not repeat,
For every boy that runs the street
Has heard it told, and preached and sung
Since first "our little Dug" was stung
    By Lincoln.

Enough for us to mention here—
That selfsame Rail will prove the bier
To bear the quondam Giant through
The ranks which he could not subdue.
    Abe Lincoln.

The foe may storm, and foam and fret;
Truth's stalwart arm shall conquer yet,
And after years repeat the tale
Of Douglas crushed beneath that Rail.
    Abe Lincoln.

—Lin'n Peel.

THE LINCOLN WEDGE.

Tune—"Maggie Lauder."

Respectfully dedicated to Gen. Clark of the Burlington, Vermont, Times.

The Democratic log is laid
  For Lincoln's wedge to split it;
See how the op'ning rive was made,
  The moment Ab'ram hit it.

CHORUS.

(Then drive the wedge, my jolly boys,
  We'll split the log, "by thunder;"

Let's cheer "Old Abe" with heart and voice,
 Till Democrats give under.)

See how the Democrats assist
 Brave Lincoln in his splitting;
Douglas pulls with giant fist—
 Breck does the science hitting.

Petite pulls right, and Breck the left,
 And wide the rent is riving;
And now, alas, 'tis fairly reft—
 To join 't were useless striving.

We grant the stuff is much decayed
 By age and speculations,
But when by Abe in rails 'tis laid,
 'T will dry in different stations.

Each Democratic rail can then,
 Freed from its rot and harm, boys,
Be safely used by honest men,
 To fence the gen'ral farm, boys.

Then let Republicans unite,
 With vig'rous blows to drive it;
Democracy's the log in sight,—
 Ho! Lincoln's wedge will rive it.

THE WOOD-CHOPPER OF THE WEST.

Far echoing in the dim old woods
Over the prairie lands and floods,
I hear the reverberating strokes
That rive in rails the prostrate oaks.

The woodman stands, sun-covered and tall,
And weilds with giant strength the maul
That drives the wedge at every blow,
Like Thor's huge hammer, sure and slow.

And his Herculean arms will hew
The shadowing trees that hide the view
Of the grand White House from the West,
That all may see our eagle's nest.

The woodman is a pioneer,
And he will cut a pathway clear
From Illinois to Washington
Before his noble task is done.
We hear the thunder of his blows
Where the vast Mississippi flows,
And echo unto echo calls
From granite hills and mountain walls.

The monarchs of the hills and vales
Are split into protective rails
To fence within its dark domains
The curse that comes with slaves and chains.

Fence out the wrongs of power and place;
Fence in the rights of all the race;
Fence out the greedy hand that steals;
Fence in the noble heart that feels.

Fence out the tyrant and his sway;
Fence in the hero of the day;
Fence out oppression, vice and crime;
Fence in the truth from Heaven sublime.
—George W. Bungay.

STORMING THE CASTLE

184   LINCOLN'S CAMPAIGN.

STEERING THE BARK OF STATE.

CHAPTER XX.

Campaign Fun and Caricature.

ARTEMUS WARD INTERVIEWING LINCOLN.

I hiv no politics. Nary a one. I'm not in the bisness. If I was I spose I should holler versiffrusly in the streets at nite and go home to Betsey Jane smellin of coal ile and gin in the mornin. I should go to the Poles arly. I should stay there all day. I should see to it that my nabers was thar. I should git carriages to take the kripples, the infirm and the indignant thar. I should be on guard agin frauds and sich. I should be on the lookout for the infamus lise of the enemy, got up jes be4 elecshun for perlitical effeck. When all was over and my candydate was elected I should move heving & arth—so to speak—until I got orfice, which if I didn't get a orfice I should turn round and abooze the Administration with all my mite and maine. But I'm not in the bisness. I'm in a far more respectful bisness nor what pollertics is. I wouldn't give two cents to be a Congresser. The wuss insult I ever received was when sertain citizens of Baldinsville axed me to run fur the Legislater. Sez I, "My frends, dostest think I'd stoop to that there?" They turned as white as a sheet. I spoke in my most orfullest tones, & they knowd I wasn't to be trifled with. They slunked out of site to onct.

There4, hevin no politics, I made bold to visit Old Abe at his humsted in Springfield. I found the old feller in his parler, surrounded by a perfeck sworm of orfice seekers. Knowin he had been capting of a flat boat on the roarin Mississippy I thought I'd address him in sailor lingo, so sez I, "Old Abe, ahoy! Let out yer main-suls, reef hum the forecastle & throw yer jib-poop overboard! Shiver my timbers, my harty!" (N. B.—This is ginuine mariner langwidge. I know, becawz I've seen sailor plays acted out by them New York theater fellers.) Old Abe lookt up quite cross & sez, "Send in yer petition by & by. I can't possibly look at it now. Indeed, I can't. It's onpossible, sir!"

"Mr. Linkin, who do you spect I air?" sed I. "A orfice-seeker, to be sure," sed he. "Well, sir," sed I, "You's never more mistaken in your life. You haint got a orfice I'd take under no circumstances. I'm A. Ward. Wax figgers is my perfeshun. I'm the father of Twins, and they look like me—both of them. I cum to pay a frendly visit to the President eleck of the United States. If so be you wants to see me say so—if not, say so, & I'm orf like a jug handle."

"Mr. Ward, sit down. I am glad to see you, sir."

"Repose in Abraham's Buzzum!" said one of the orfice

seekers, his idea being to git orf a goak at my expense.

"Wall," sez I, "ef all you fellers repose in that there Buzzum there'll be mity poor nussin for sum of you!"

whereupon Old Abe buttoned his weskit clear up and blusht like a maiding of sweet 16. Jest at this point of the conversation another swarm of orfice seekers arrove & cum pilin into the parler. Sum wanted post orfices, sum wanted collectorships, sum wanted furrin missions, and all wanted sumthin. I thought Old Abe would go crazy. He hadn't more than had time to shake hands with 'em, before another tremenjis crowd cum porcin onto his premises. His house and dooryard was perfeckly overflowed with orfice seekers, all clameruss for a immejit interview with Old Abe. One man from Ohio, who had about seven inches of corn whiskey in him, mistook me fur Old Abe and addresst me as "The Pra-hayrie Flower of the West!" Thinks I you want a offis putty bad. Another man with a gold-headed cane and a red nose told Abe he was "a sekind Washington and the Pride of the Boundless West!"

Sez I, "Square, you wouldn't take a small post-offis if you could git it, would you?"

Sez he, "A patrit is abuv them things, sir!"

"There's a putty big crop of patrits this season, aint there, Square?" sez I, when another crowd of ofiis seekers pored in. The house, dooryard, barn & woodshed was now all full, and when another crowd cum I told 'em not to go away for want of room, as the hog-pen was still empty. One patrit from a small town in Mishygan went up on top the house, got into the chimney and slid down into the parler, where Old Abe was endeverin to keep the hungry pack of offiss-seekers from chawin him up alive without benefit of clergy. The minit he reached the fire place he jumpt up, brusht the soot out of his eyes, and yelled: "Don't make any pintment of Spunkville Post-office till you've read my papers. All the respectful men

OUR GREAT ICEBERG MELTING AWAY.

190   LINCOLN'S CAMPAIGN:

THE PERILOUS VOYAGE TO THE WHITE HOUSE.

in our town is signers to that there dockyment!"

"Good God!" cride Old Abe, "they cum upon me frum the skize—down the chimneys, and from the bowels of the yearth!" He hadn't more'n got them words out of his delikit mouth before two fat offiss-seekers from Wisconsin, in endeaverin to crawl atween his legs for the purpose of applyin for the tollgateship of Milwawky, upsot the President elcck & he would hev gone sprawlin into the fire place if I hadn't caught him in these arms. But I hadn't more'n stood him up strate, before another man cum crashing down the chimney, his head striking me vilently agin the inards and prostratin my voluptoous form onto the floor. "Mr. Linkin," shoutid the infatooated being, "my papers are signed by every clergyman in our town, and likewise the schoolmaster!"

Sez I, "You egrejis ass," gitin up & brushin the dust from my eyes, "I'll sign your papers with this bunch of bones, if you don't be a little more keerful how you make my bredbasket a depot in the futer. How do you like that air perfumery?" sez I, shuving my fist under his nose. "Them's the kind of papers I give you! Them's the papers you want?"

"But I workt hard for the ticket; I toiled night and day! The patrit should be rewarded!"

"Virtoo," sed I, holdin the infatooated man by the coat collar—"virtoo, sir, is its own reward. Look at me!" He did look at me, and qualed be4 my gase. "The fact is," I continued, lookin' round upon the hungry crowd, "There is scarcely a offiss for evry ile lamp carried round durin' this campane. I wish there was. I wish there was furrin missions to be filled on varis lonely islands where eppydemics rage incessantly, and if I was in Old Abe's place, I'd send every mother's son of you to them. What air you here for?" I continnered, warmin up considerable. "Can't you give Abe a minit's peace? Don't you see he's worried most to death? Go home, you miserable men, go home and till the sile! Go to peddlin tinware—go to choppin wood—go to bilin soap—stuff sassengers—black boots—git a clerkship on some respectable manure cart—go round as original Swiss Bell Ringers—becum 'original and only' Campbell Minstrels—go to lecturin at 50 dollars a nite—imbark in the peanut bisness—write for the Ledger—saw off your legs and go round givin concerts, with techin appeals to a charitable public, printed on your handbills—anything for a honest livin', but don't cum round here drivin Old Abe crazy by your outragus cuttings up! Go home, stand not upon the order of your goin', but go to onct! If in five minits from this time," sez I, pullin out my new sixteen dollar huntin cased watch, and brandishin' it before their eyes, "Ef in five minits from this time a single sole of you remains on these premises I'll go out to my cage near by, and let my Boy Constructor loose! & if he gits amung you, you'll think Old Solferino hus cum again and no mistake!" You ought to hev seen them

THE POLITICAL REVOLUTION OF 1860.

A WINNER FROM WAY-BACK.

"THREE TO ONE YOU DON'T GET IT."

(Variation on the popular interpretation of the meaning of the Pawnbrokers' sign.)

scamper, Mr. Fair. They orf as the Satun hisself was arter them with a red hot ten pronged pitchfork. In five minits the premises was clear.

"How kin I ever repay you, Mr. Ward, for your kindness?" sed Old Abe, advancin and shakin me warmly by the hand. "How kin I ever repay you, sir?"

"By givin the whole country a good sound administration. By porein ile upon the troubled waters, North and South. By persooin' a patriotic, firm and just course, and then if any State wants to secede, let 'em Sesesh!"

"How 'bout my Cabinet Ministre, Ward?" sed Abe.

"Fill it up with showmen, sir. Showmen is devoid of politics. They hain't got a durn principle! They know how to cater to the public. They know what the public wants, North & South. Showmen, sir, is honest men. Ef you doubt their literary ability, look at their posters, and see small bills! Ef you want a Cabinet as is a Cabinet fill it up with Showmen, but don't call on me. The moral wax figger perfeshun mustn't be permitted to go down while there's a drop of blood in these vains! A. Linkin, I wish you well! Ef Powers or Walcutt was to pick out a model for a beautiful man, I scarcely think they'd sculp you; but ef you do the fair thing by your country you'll make as putty a angel as any of us, or any other man! A. Linkin, use the talents which Nature has put into you judishusly and firmly, and all will be well! A. Linken, adoo!"

He shook me cordyully by the hand—we exchanged picters, so we could gaze upon each other's liniments when far away from one another—he at the hellum of the ship of State, and I at the hellum of the show bizness—admittance only 15 cents.

Artemus Ward.

From Vanity Fair, December 8, 1860.

STRAY SHOTS.

While the rails of our steam highways rest upon "sleepers," Lincoln's political rails are borne up by "Wide-awakes."

* * *

An Ill-an'-noisy affair:
The Chicago convention.

* * *

One from the Mining Districts:
Pennsylvania, always influenced by its Iron interests, is sure to go for Lincoln, simply because he is the "Rail Candidate."

* * *

Democratic Matter:
"We Polked them in 1844; we Pierced them in 1852; we Bucked them in 1856; we're Breck-ing now, and our grave is Dug!"

* * *

Mr. Lincoln was successful because the ladies were in favor of hy-men.

THE POLITICAL REVOLUTION OF 1860.

THE GREAT EXHIBITION OF 1860.

The Long and Short of the Presidential Canvass:
Lincoln and Douglas.

* * *

When we put Lincoln in, we shall know what is what;
When we put Douglas in, we shall know how to squat;
When we put Breckinridge in, there'll be powder and smoke;
When we choose Bell and Everett, 'twill be a good joke;
And when Houston first reaches the goal on the rails,
It will doubtless rain larks with salt on their tails.
Now, as knowledge, and squatting, and powder, and jokes,
And as good showers of larks would blessings be to folks,
Whosoever comes in of a gay brotherhood,
You may feel pretty sure he will do us some good.

* * *

It has been noticed by political sign-watchers, that, in the precise ratio that a candidate comes down, his prospects come up.

* * *

Why is Stephen A. Douglas a greater man than Abe Lincoln? Because the former split a party, while the latter only split a rail.

* * *

When is a Wide-Awake like a poultry dealer? When he has a cap(e)-on.

* * *

Tribute to the "six feet four:"
"Lincoln sweetness long drawn out."

* * *

Republican delicacy of the season: Rail birds.

* * *

What the Republicans depend upon for success—Rail-lery.

* * *

The Republicans propose to change the ornithological symbol of America by withdrawing the Eagle and substituting the Rail.

THE POLITICAL REVOLUTION OF 1860.

THE POLITICAL GYMNASIUM.

200 LINCOLN'S CAMPAIGN:

"For President, A. S. Dugass,
For Vice President, H. V. Johnsing, ALL Right."

* * *

"Douglas forever, never Beet yit."

* * *

DOUGLAS AND HIS MOUNT.

* * *

At St. Joseph, Missouri, before the election, the Douglas men paraded with such banners as these:

"Old Abe cut his tow so, when he split that last rale, he kant run fast enough to keep sight of the little Giant."

* * *

TAKING THE STUMP "OB STEPHEN IN SEARCH OF HIS MOTHER."

SPLIT VERSUS SPLIT.

"Abe and his rails." O worse than idle tale—
We Democrats can lay you on the shelf.
Boast of a man who's only split a rail?
Our good old party's gone and split itself!

* * *

THE NEW GULLIVER;
OR SWALLOWING A "LITTLE GIANT."

* * *

"Jones, did you see that splendid half bust of Mr. Douglas, when you were in New York?" "Yes; but I've seen a finer one since in Pennsylvania. It was a full bust."

* * *

THE NATIONAL GAME. THREE "OUTS" AND ONE "RUN."

DIED.—At Charleston, South Carolina, on the 3rd instant, the old and well-known horse Democracy.

The above named horse was sired by Thomas Jefferson and dam(n)ed by Stephen A. Douglas.

* * *

Lincoln and Douglas are a great pair of splitters. Lincoln once followed the business of splitting rails, and Douglas has now split his party.—*Louisville Journal.*

* * *

DEMOCRAT ON THE FENCE.
"I daren't jump, and I can't git here. What the deuce shall I do."

* * *

Mr. Lincoln is an unselfish man. He has made many rails, and yet he never was on the fence in his life.—*Boston Traveller.*

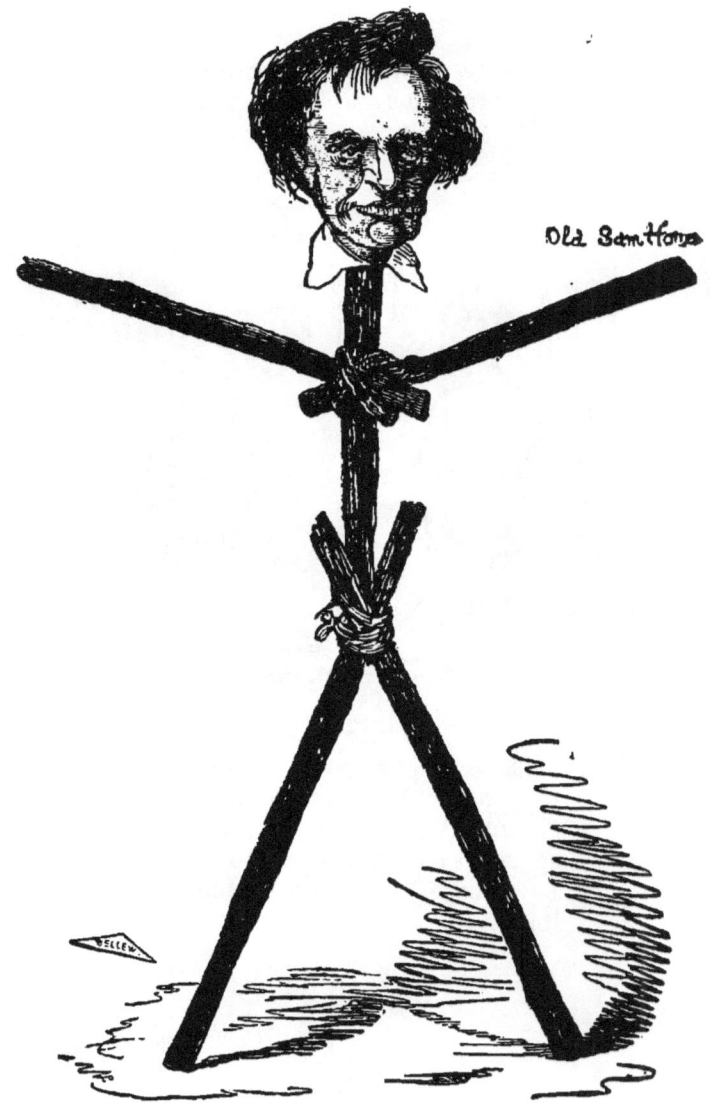

A "RAIL" OLD WESTERN GENTLEMAN.

Brown won't vote for Lincoln, because he thinks if he is elected the presidential office would be probably Abe-used.

* * *

* * *

First Boy—"'S your father goin' to run for President this year?" Second Boy—"Guess so; he says he may as well—everybody else is doin' it."—Comic Monthly, 1860.

THE SPLIT IN THE DEMOCRATIC PARTY.

CAMPAIGN OF 1896.

PRESIDENTIAL POSSIBILITIES.

Republicans.

WILLIAM McKINLEY.

William McKinley was born on January 29, 1843, at Niles, Trumbull County, Ohio, where his father was interested in one of the early iron furnaces of that section. He was educated in the common schools and at the Poland Academy, and in 1860, at the age of 17, entered Allegheny College. Taken sick early in the term, he returned home, and that winter, following the example of so many great Americans, taught a country school near Poland. His duties ended in April, 1861, and it was his intention to go back to Allegheny College that fall. But while this young country boy had been teaching his little school, great and important events were transpiring. A new school opened its doors to the youth of the North—the grim school of war.

Most Prominent Republican Presidential Possibilities, 1896

Most Prominent Democratic Presidential Possibilities, 1896

In June the Twenty-third regiment of Ohio Volunteers was organized at Columbus. Its first Colonel was William S. Rosecrans, afterwards Major General and Commander of the Department of the Cumberland. Its Lieutenant Colonel was Stanley Matthews, who became United States Senator and Justice of the Supreme Court. Its Major was Rutherford B. Hayes, later thrice Governor of Ohio, and President of the United States. And there marched in the ranks of Company E, an 18-year-old private, whose name was William McKinley. After Antietam he was promoted to Second Lieutenant. Subsequent promotion came, and he served on the brigade and division staff of General R. B. Hayes, part of the time as aide-de-camp. Then he was detailed as Acting Assistant Adjutant General on the staff of General George Crook, and was with Sheridan in his great campaign through the Shenandoah Valley.

One of the most cherished of his possessions is a document, worn and time-stained now. It is his commission as Brevet Major of the United States Volunteers, given in 1864, "for gallant and meritorious services at the battles of Opequan, Cedar Creek and Fisher's Hill," and is signed "A. Lincoln."

He was present when Lee surrendered to Grant at Appomatox. In September, 1865, he was mustered out, after over five years' continuous service as a soldier. He entered the army as a private. He left it a Major of United States Volunteers by brevet. Mr. McKinley was 22 when he returned to Ohio and civil life. His four years' service had given him a taste for army life, and but for his father's opposition he might have entered the regular army, as General Carroll desired him to do. However, he finally chose civil life, studied law with Charles E. Glidden and David Wilson, of Mahoning County, took a course at the Albany (N. Y.) Law School, and in 1867 was admitted to the bar, and located at Canton, Stark County, ever since his home. Two years later he ran for Prosecuting Attorney of the county. Stark County was Democratic, but McKinley was elected and served two years. Meanwhile, he became active in politics. He took the stump for his party and soon made himself a power among the people.

On January 25, 1871, he was married to Miss Ida Saxton, daughter of James A. Saxton, a prominent citizen of Canton.

In 1876 he was proposed as a candidate for Congress. The sitting Congressman, L. D. Woodworth, of Mahoning, Judge Frease and several other Republicans, three of them from his own county, were opponents for the nomination. In Stark County delegates to the Congressional Convention were elected by a popular vote. McKinley carried every township in the county but one, and that was but a single delegate. In the other counties he

THE POLITICAL REVOLUTION OF 1860. 211

was almost equally successful, and the primaries gave him a majority of all the delegates in the district. He was nominated on the first ballot over all the other candidates and duly elected.

For fourteen years he represented the district of which Stark County was a part—not the same district, for the Democrats did not relish the prominent part he was playing in Congress, and "gerrymandered" him three times. His record in Congress and the fame he acquired all over the world through his fathering the famous tariff bill that bore his name, are matters of history that need no comments. In 1890 Mr. McKinley entered a fourth Congressional contest against ex-Lieutenant Governor Warwick, a prominent and popular Democrat. Not, perhaps, since Abraham Lincoln contested Illinois for the Senatorship against Stephen A. Douglas, has there been, in one sense, a local political struggle which the whole country watched with such intense interest.

Despite the heavy odds against him, Major McKinley was beaten by a beggarly 303 votes, and that on the fullest vote ever cast in the district. He polled 2,500 more votes than had been given Harrison in 1888. This defeat in 1890 took him out of Congress. It made him Governor of Ohio in 1891. Two years later he was again unanimously nominated, and it was then that he received the highest vote ever cast for any candidate in Ohio.

THOMAS B. REED.

Thomas Brackett Reed was born in Portland, Maine, on October 18, 1839. The common schools of the city gave him his early education, and it was finished at Bowdoin College. Here he graduated in 1860, among the first in his class, and taking the highest honors open to a Bowdoin student—the prize for excellence in English composition. His college days ended, he began to teach in a Portland high school, studying law meantime. In 1863 he went to California, intending to make his home in that far-off State. There he taught school, too, and began the practice of law, but family reasons called him back to Portland before he had been a year on the Pacific slope. In April, 1864, he was appointed Acting Assistant Paymaster in the United States Navy, and assigned to duty on the gunboat Sybil, commanded by Lieutenant H. H. Gorringe. Mr. Reed was discharged from the United States service in August, 1865, and returned to Portland. He was admitted to the bar of his native county of Cumberland, and his civil career began in earneset. He soon became active as a Republican, so active and so favorably was he regarded that, in 1868, his party nominated him for the Maine House of Representatives. He was elected, and, so excellent was the legal reputation he had established in but three years' practice, that he was put on the Judiciary Committee.

The Maine Republicans saw that they had found the right sort of a Representative, and promptly re-elected him in 1869, and promoted him to the Senate in 1870. In Maine, the Legislature elects every State officer except the Governor, and so thoroughly had the young legislator commended himself to the whole State, as well as to his immediate constituents, that he was chosen Attorney General, and resigned his Senatorship to take his new honors. He was then but 30 years old, the youngest Attorney General the State has ever had. Attorney General Reed was in office three years. He made himself a name, both as a lawyer and public servant.

Retiring from office in 1873, he was appointed City Solicitor of Portland the next year, and in that position strengthened the popular confidence in his abilities and integrity. He was now well known, not only in his own city and county, but throughout the State.

In 1867 he became a candidate for Congress in the district composed of Cumberland and York Counties. All the influences that the united forces of the custom house and postoffice could bring to bear against him had to be overcome. The Convention met and ballotted all day, but Reed was nominated, and, in November, was elected.

Mr. Reed was re-elected in 1878, and his abilities were recognized by a place on the Judiciary Committee. Now he began to figure prominently in debate, so prominently, in fact, that when the Republican Congress elected with Garfield in 1880 met in December, 1881, he received some votes in caucus for speaker against Keifer, of Ohio, the successful candidate. He was made chairman of the Judiciary Committee in that house and was a leader on the Republican side.

His position was now established. In 1885 he won the honor of the caucus nomination for the Speakership over Frank Hiscock, of New York, and that without asking a man to vote for him unless spoken to by the man himself. In 1887 he was unanimously chosen in caucus. But in both the Forty-eighth and Fiftieth Congresses the House was Democratic and Carlisle was made Speaker. Reed's turn came in 1889. That year the House was Republican, though by a bare majority. Then he had opposition for the coveted place. Major McKinley, of Ohio, Cannon, of Illinois, Henderson, of Iowa, and Burrows, of Michigan, all strong men, were aspirants, and it looked, on the surface, like a great fight. But it was not in reality. All went to Reed and he was nominated on the second ballot. The ex-Speaker was also the unanimous choice of the Republican House caucus in the Fifty-second and Fifty-third Congresses, in both of which, and especially the latter, the House was Democratic.

The memorable Fifty-first Congress met on December 2, 1889. Thomas B. Reed was elected Speaker, receiving 166 votes to 154 to John G. Carlisle. On assuming the chair he said:

"I thank you for the high office which your voices have bestowed upon me. It would be impossible not to be moved by its dignity and honor. Yet you may well imagine that I am at this moment more impressed by its responsibilities and duties. Under our system of government as it has been developed these responsibilities and duties are both political and parliamentary. So far as the duties are political, I sincerely hope they may be performed with a proper sense of what is due to this whole country. So far as they are parliamentary, I hope, with equal sincerity, that they may be performed with a proper sense of what is due to both sides of this chamber."

Mr. Reed's powers as a leader were never better tested as the leader of a minority than during the sessions of the Fifty-second and Fifty-third Congresses. Especially were his powers manifested during the struggles over the Wilson tariff bill and the Bland seigniorage bills in the eventful session of 1894. It was wonderful to see Reed's control of his party in the House. He was equal to every emergency. No matter how sudden the turn in affairs, how critical the occasion, his keen mind at once discerned the proper course, and with a wave of his hand he called the Republicans to their feet or bade them keep their seats.

The family consists of Mr. and Mrs. Reed and one daughter, Miss Catherine. Mrs. Reed was the daughter of the Rev. Mr. Merrill, formerly a pastor of a Congregational church in Portland, and that is the church which the Speaker and his family attend when at home. He still practices law, but of late years his public duties have largely debarred him from those of his profession. Mr. Reed is a man of but moderate circumstances.

In Portland, where his whole life has been spent, he is very popular. Democratic in his manners, genial, affable and pleasant, everybody knows and everybody respects him. A man of strong opinions, he speaks his mind freely, never compromises anything merely to be agreeable, but he is always square and fair, and people know that he means what he says.

LEVI P. MORTON.

Levi P. Morton was born in Shoreham, Vt., May 16, 1824. When 15 years old he clerked in a store at Enfield, Mass., after which he became proprietor of a store at Hanover, N. H. Displaying unusual business qualifications, he was offered an important clerkship in the firm of James M. Beebe & Co., of Boston.

Mr. Morton accepted this offer and sold out his store and moved to Boston. He was afterward made a member of the firm. In 1853 he removed to New York, where the firm opened a branch and placed Mr. Morton in charge. In 1856 the house of Morton, Grinnell & Co., dry goods commission merchants and importers, was established at No. 64 Broadway. When the rebellion broke out there were a number of young men in his employ who belonged to militia regiments and who responded to the call for ninety days' service immediately after the attack on Fort Sumter. All these gentlemen took their place in the ranks, and their places in the store were reserved for them while they were absent, and their pay continued throughout that period. When the war commenced, it was impossible to make collections in the South. As a large proportion of the trade of the firm of Morton, Grinnell & Co. was in the Southern States, the firm was compelled to suspend. A satisfactory settlement was made and the firm resumed business in the latter part of 1861. In 1863 the banking firm of L. P. Morton & Co. was established. The firm was now known as Morton, Bliss & Co. in New York, and Morton, Rose & Co. in London. The firms of which Mr. Morton is the head were active in the payment of the Geneva award of $15,500,000 and the Halifax fishery award of $5,500,000. In 1876 Mr. Morton was nominated for Congress by the Republicans of the Eleventh district of New York. He was defeated, although he reduced the Democratic majority by hundreds of votes. He was again nominated in 1878 for the same office, and received a larger majority than the total number of votes cast for his Democratic opponent, Ben F. Willis, the sitting member.

In 1880 he declined the nomination for Vice President on the Republican ticket with President Garfield. Mr. Morton was appointed honorary commissioner to the Paris Exposition in 1878. He filled the office of Minister to France from 1881 to 1885. He made a good impression at the French capital and secured the esteem and good will of many of the leading men of France. Through his intercessions the restrictions upon the importation of American pork were removed. Mr. Morton was nominated for the Vice Presidency of the United States in 1888 on the ticket with President Harrison. He performed the functions of that high office to the entire satisfaction of both parties in the Senate. At the close of his Vice Presidential term Mr. Morton withdrew again from public life and attended to his private business. In 1894 he was elected Governor of New York.

Mr. Morton was twice married. His first wife was Miss Lucy Kimball, of Flatlands, Long Island. She bore him no children, and in a few years he was a widower.

His present wife was Miss Street, of New York, and five daughters are the result of this marriage.

The benevolent side of Mr. Morton's nature, as was the case with Mr. Lincoln, is always ready to manifest itself. His action during the period of the Irish famine several years ago resulted in the forwarding of a shipload of provisions from America to the sufferers, but it was done with the express desire that his name should be withheld from public notice. His contributions to the yellow fever sufferers of the South will probably never be correctly estimated, though it is known that he was a large donor to the funds raised for relief at that time.

WILLIAM B. ALLISON.

William B. Allison, of Dubuque, Iowa, was born in Perry, Wayne County, Ohio, March 2, 1829. He spent his early years on a farm, and grew up like other country boys. He was sent to the district school, a school house in the woods, at an early age, and made remarkable progress. His father sent him, at the age of 16, to an academy at Wooster, Ohio. He remained in that school during two years, after which he was sent to Allegheny College, Meadville, Penn. He taught school for one winter; then attended the Western Reserve College, Ohio. He had toiled and struggled with the toiling and struggling masses who constitute the strength and the real greatness of this country. He studied law and practiced in Ohio until he moved to Iowa in 1857. In 1854 he married Miss Anna Carter, the daughter of Hon. Daniel Carter, of Ashland, Ohio, a man of prominence in that day. She died in 1860. He married Miss Mary Nealley in 1873. Mr. Allison learned early in life to take an interest in political affairs. He was a delegate from Ashland County to the state convention which nominated Salmon P. Chase for Governor of Ohio. He was an active worker and supporter of Fremont for President in 1856. He was honored by being sent as a delegate to the National Republican Convention which nominated Abraham Lincoln in 1860, and was selected as one of the secretaries of that convention. He was the first to cast up the long column of votes and to announce to the presiding officer that Lincoln had received the required number of votes and was therefore the nominee of the convention.

When President Lincoln issued his second call for troops, during the summer of 1861, for 30,000 men, Gov. Samuel J. Kirkwood thought of the sincere and successful young man whom he had known in Ohio, as well as in Iowa. He placed Mr. Allison on his staff, with the rank of Lieutenant-Colonel, and gave him full authority to raise regiments in northeastern Iowa and to equip them for service in the field. He raised in all four regiments. He was elected as a representative in Congress and took his seat Dec. 3, 1863. James G. Blaine and James A. Garfield took their seats in the same house. The war delegation in congress from Iowa was one of great strength and gave the young state immediate standing in the national councils. Mr. Allison was, as far as can be ascertained, the first to advocate the idea of the soldiers at the front being allowed to cast their votes. An extra session of the Iowa Legislature was called in 1862, authorizing the soldiers to vote in the field. To Mr. Allison belongs much credit for the patriotic stand taken, so just to the soldiers under arms.

Mr. Allison was three times re-elected, serving in the House from 1863 to 1871. He declined a renomination in 1870. At the commencement of his second term in Congress, he was placed on the Ways and Means Committee, and remained there during the rest of his service in the House. In 1872 Mr. Allison was elected to the United States Senate, succeeding Senator James Harlan. He took his seat March 4, 1873, and has been four times re-elected since. During it all he has grown in the confidence and affection of the people of the State, so that at the last re-election there was no opposition against him.

During all the years he has stood the steadfast advocate of what he believed was the right. He has devoted himself not to "one," but to "all" National matters. He has been a Senator of broad vision and sound judgment.

He came into most marked prominence in 1876, when he offered in the Finance Committee two amendments to the Bland silver bill. The Bland bill was a free and unlimited coinage measure. The bill had passed the House. Mr. Allison believed it was fraught with danger. His amendments completely changed the effects of the bill. It turned its influence in exactly the opposite direction. The two important features of the amendments were the coinage of silver on Government account, and the committal of the Government to the policy of the use of both gold and silver as coinage metals, looking to an ultimate international agreement as to a ratio of coinage.

Mr. Allison was twice tendered a seat in the Cabinet, first by President Garfield, and next by President Harrison. Domestic cares prevented him from accepting this much prized position. Senator Allison is, from every point of view, a man. He is that rare combination of simplicity and strength; of frankness and reserve; of gentleness and ruggedness, which appeals to the eye and to the heart, no less than to the intellect. He is strong of body, big of head, and warm of heart.

SHELBY M. CULLOM.

Shelby Moore Cullom, son of Richard N. Cullom and Elizabeth C. Cullom, was born in Monticello, Wayne County, Kentucky, November 22, 1829. His father removed to Tazewell County, Illinois, the following year, so that young Shelby narrowly missed being a native of his adopted State. Hon. R. N. Cullom was a prominent and influential Whig in his time, and frequently represented his district in both houses of the General Assembly. He was a farmer, and the embryo U. S. Senator was early accustomed to the homely fare and rough work incident to farm life in a comparatively new country. His hands soon learned to swing the ax and guide the plow, and it was in such pursuits as these that he acquired that physical strength which he devoted to public service.

During his boyhood days, country schools were considered sufficient to equip a young man for the battle of life. Shelby M. Cullom, however, was not content with this. He decided to devote himself to the law, and was enabled to spend two years in study at Rock River Seminary, Mt. Morris. In order to maintain himself, he found it necessary to devote some time to teaching. In 1853 he entered the office of Stuart & Edwards, at Springfield, and began the study of law.

He was admitted to the bar in 1855. Soon after this, he was elected City Attorney in Springfield, and soon entered a broader field of practice.

In 1856 Mr. Cullom made his debut into political life by entering the Lower House of the General Assembly. He had always been in sympathy with the principles of the Republican party, and being a warm personal friend of

Abraham Lincoln, was one of his strongest supporters for the United States Senate in 1858. In 1860 he was re-elected to the Legislature.

The Republicans, now for the first time, secured ascendency in the Legislature, and Mr. Cullom was elected Speaker.

In 1864 he received the Republican nomination for Congress, and succeeded in overcoming a Democratic majority of 1,365, and transforming it into one of 1,785 in his favor.

Mr. Cullom was re-elected in 1866, and again in 1868, but in 1870 his district was lost to the Republicans.

In 1872 he was again returned as a member of the State Legislature, and elected Speaker. In 1874 he was, for the fourth time, the chosen representative of Sangamon County in the General Assembly. When the State Convention met in the Centennial year, it was found that a large majority of the delegates were favorable to his nomination for the Governorship. He was duly elected the following November.

He was re-elected in 1880, the first instance of a re-election to a second consecutive term in the history of the State.

At the expiration of the term of David Davis as United States Senator from Illinois, in March, 1883, Governor Cullom was elected to succeed him. He was re-elected U. S. Senator in 1889 and 1895.

Shelby M. Cullom has served eight years in the Legislature of the State, during four years of which he presided as Speaker of the House; six years in the House of Representatives at Washington; upwards of six years as Governor of Illinois, and up to this time nearly fourteen years in the Senate of the United States, making over a third of a century in the public service of his district and State.

CHARLES F. MANDERSON.

Charles Frederick Manderson was born of Scotch-Irish ancestry in Philadelphia, Penn., February 9, 1837, and received his education in the schools of his native city. At the age of 19 he removed to Canton, Stark County, Ohio, where he studied law and was admitted to the bar in 1859. In the spring of 1860 he was elected City Solicitor of Canton, Ohio, and was re-elected the next year.

On the day of the receipt of the news of the firing on Fort Sumter, he enlisted as a private with Captain James Wallace, of the Canton Zouaves, an independent company in which he had been a corporal. Receiving permission from Governor Dennison, with Samuel Beatty, an old Mexican soldier, then Sheriff of Stark County, to raise a company of infantry, they recruited a full company in one day in April, 1861, Manderson being elected and commissioned First Lieutenant. In May, 1861, Beatty, the Captain, being made Colonel of the Nineteenth Ohio Infantry, Manderson became Captain of Company "A" of that Regiment.

The Regiment participated with great credit in the first field battle of the war, on the 11th day of July, 1861. Captain Manderson received special mention in the official reports of this battle. In August, 1861, he re-enlisted his company for three years, or during the war, and in this service he rose through the grades of Major, Lieutenant Colonel, and Colonel of the Nineteenth Ohio Infantry, and on January 1st, 1864, over 400 of the survivors of his Regiment re-enlisted with him as veteran volunteers.

He was in command of the Nineteenth Ohio Infantry in all its engagements up to and including the battle of Lovejoy's Station, on September 2nd, 1864. On that day Colonel Manderson, then in command of a demi-brigade, was severely wounded. At the battle of Stone River, or Murfreesboro, the Regiment lost in killed and wounded 213 men out of 449 taken into the engagement, or 44 per cent.

He was compelled to resign the service from those wounds in April, 1865. Previous to his resignation he was brevetted Brigadier General of Volunteers U. S. A., "for long, faithful, gallant and meritorious service during the War of Rebellion."

Returning to Canton, Ohio, he resumed the practice of law, and was twice elected District Attorney of Stark County, declining a nomination for a third term.

In November, 1869, he removed to Omaha, Neb., where he still resides, and where he quickly became prominent in legal and political affairs. He was a member of the Nebraska State Constitutional Convention of 1871, and also that of 1874, being elected without opposition. He served as City Attorney of Omaha, Nebraska, for over six years. He has been an active comrade in the Grand Army of the Republic, and for three years was commander of the Military Order of the Loyal Legion of the District of Columbia. He was elected United States Senator as a Republican to succeed Alvin Saunders, his term commencing March 4th, 1883. He was re-elected to the Senate in 1888 without opposition and with exceptional and unprecedented marks of approval from the Legislature of Nebraska. His term expired March 3rd, 1895, and he declined to be a candidate for a third term, announcing publicly his intention to retire from public life.

In the second session of the Fifty-first Congress he was elected by the U. S. Senate as its President Pro Tempore without opposition, it having been declared by the Senate after full debate to be a continuing office. This unanimous election to the Presidency of the Senate was without a precedent, and was the highest compliment that could be paid by that body to one of its members.

General Manderson occupies now the position of General Solicitor of the Burlington System of Railroads west of the Missouri River, continuing his residence at Omaha, Nebraska.

MATTHEW S. QUAY.

Matthew Stanley Quay was born at Dillsburg, York County, Pennsylvania, September 30, 1833. He graduated

from Jefferson College, and subsequently studied law at Pittsburg, where he was admitted to the bar in 1854.

From 1855 to 1859 Mr. Quay held the elective office of prothonotary of Beaver County. When the Civil war broke out he enlisted at once in the Tenth Pennsylvania Regiment, and was appointed a First Lieutenant. Shortly afterward he was made Assistant Commissary General of the State forces, with rank of Lieutenant Colonel. Governor Andrew G. Curtin selected the brilliant young officer as his private secretary until the latter went to the front as Colonel of the One Hundred and Thirty-fourth Pennsylvania Regiment. His health having broken down, he was mustered out in 1862. Hardly on his feet again, he accepted the arduous duties of military secretary of Pennsylvania, an office just then created to meet the dire necessities of the times.

Mr. Quay was elected to the Legislature of his State in 1864, 1865 and 1866. In 1869 he established the "Beaver Radical," a valiant and uncompromisingly Republican sheet. From 1873 to 1878 he occupied the high elective office of Secretary of the Commonwealth of Pennsylvania. After one year's term as Recorder of Philadelphia, Mr. Quay was re-elected Secretary (1879). In 1885 the largest vote ever recorded in the State (for that office) made him State Treasurer. Finally, in 1887 and again in 1893, he was elected a United States Senator for his native State.

Democrats.

GROVER CLEVELAND.

Grover Cleveland was born in the town of Caldwell, Essex County, New Jersey, on the 18th day of March, 1837. He is a descendant of an English family, which has been in this country two hundred years. The family is noted for its piety and religious zeal, having had for many generations distinguished representatives in the clerical profession. Grover Cleveland's father was educated for the ministry, and was of the Presbyterian faith. Mr. Cleveland's educational facilities and opportunities were rather limited, consisting of a chance to attend the common schools, and later for a brief period an Academy at Clinton, Oneida County, N. Y. After leaving the Academy, in his 17th year, he became a clerk and an assistant teacher in an institution for the blind in New York City. In 1855, with a companion, he started for Cleveland, Ohio. On his way there he stopped at Buffalo, N. Y., to visit an uncle, Lewis F. Allen, who used his best endeavors to dissuade his nephew from going farther. To make his arguments and entreaties effective, he offered Grover a clerkship. As work was what young Cleveland desired, he, of course, decided to stay. Having determined upon the law as a profession, it wasn't long before he made arrangements to become a law student in the office of Rogers,

Brown & Rogers. In 1859 he was admitted to the bar, passing most creditably a rigid examination. He continued with his preceptors nearly four years, which were a period of thorough study and legal experience. He was appointed in January, 1863, Assistant District Attorney for the County of Erie, which position he filled for three years. In 1865 he was nominated by the Democratic County Convention for District Attorney, to succeed Mr. Torrance, but was defeated by Hon. Lyman K. Bass. Mr. Cleveland formed a law copartnership with Isaac V. Vanderpool, January 1, 1866, which was continued until 1869. He then became a member of the firm of Lanning, Cleveland & Folsom. In November, 1870, Mr. Cleveland was chosen Sheriff of Erie County, and at the close of his term of office became a member of the firm of Bass, Cleveland & Bissell. Lyman K. Bass, his personal friend and political antagonist, was forced to retire from the firm on account of failing health, the firm then becoming Cleveland & Bissell. Mr. Bissell was in Mr. Cleveland's second Cabinet as Postmaster General. The firm was prosperous, and considered the strongest and brainiest in Western New York. In 1881 Mr. Cleveland was chosen Mayor of Buffalo, receiving a majority of 3,500. He defeated the Republican candidate for Governor of New York, Charles J. Folger, by a plurality of 192,854, and was inaugurated Governor in 1883, dispensing with the usual ceremony and parade. He was nominated at Chicago.

Ill., July 11, 1884, receiving 683 votes out of 820. A two-thirds vote (557) was necessary to a nomination. Mr. Cleveland was elected President, defeating James G. Blaine by 37 electoral votes. The marriage of President Cleveland and Miss Frances Folsom, of Buffalo, N. Y., took place on Wednesday, June 2, 1886, in the White House, at a few minutes past 7 in the evening.

As a candidate for re-election in 1888, Mr. Cleveland was beaten by Benjamin Harrison, receiving only 168 electoral votes, against 233 given to his successful antagonist.

In 1892 he became, anew, the candidate of his party, and was elected President of the United States for a second term. The vote stood: Grover Cleveland, 277; Benjamin Harrison, 145; James B. Weaver (Populist), 22.

Should Mr. Cleveland be the candidate of his party in 1896, it would be the first case on record of a Presidential candidate running for a third term.

JOHN G. CARLISLE.

John Griffin Carlisle, of Covington, Ky., was born in Campbell (now Kenton) County, Ky. September 5, 1835. His father, Lilbon Hardin Carlisle, was born April 22, 1811, and in the latter part of 1833 was married in Washington, Mason County, Ky., to Mary Reynolds, who was born in Catskill, N. Y. John G. Carlisle was the eldest child, and immediately after the death of his father in 1853 began the cares and battles of life by assisting his mother in the supervision and rearing of a large family. Mr. Carlisle, like many of our sturdy men, began his life in immediate contact with the soil. His early education was obtained in and near his home, embracing such branches as were taught in the common schools. He disliked manual labor, and especially field labor, and for this reason some, persons called him a lazy boy. His activities were mental rather than physical, and he always was very fond of books. In 1855 he went to Covington, Ky., to seek a situation as a teacher in the public schools. One of the examiners said of him: "I regarded John G. Carlisle's attainments, with his limited opportunities and at his time of life, among the solidest ever investigated by any board of school examiners."

In 1856 Mr. Carlisle became a student of the law under the tutelage of Hon. John W. Stevenson, who was subsequently Governor of Kentucky and United States Senator. He was admitted to the bar in March, 1858. On January 15, 1857, he was married to Miss Mary Jane Goodson, a daughter of Hon. John A. Goodson, a prominent citizen of Kentucky. Five children were born to them, only two of whom—William K. and Lilbon Logan—survive.

In 1859 Mr. Carlisle was elected a Representative to the Kentucky Legislature for two years. At the outbreak of the civil war Kentucky was in a state of bitter dissension. Families were divided, brother enlisted to fight against brother, and father against son. There was a strong secession party which made bold efforts to get control of the State. Mr. Carlisle did not believe that the States had the constitutional right to secede, and from the first was a consistent opponent of all attempts to call a convention for the purpose of taking the State out of the Union. This was a step which was destined to exert an important influence upon his career.

In 1866 he was elected to the Kentucky State Senate and at the close of the term was re-elected. During the second term he was elected Lieutenant-Governor. He was elected to the Forty-fifth Congress and remained in the House of Representatives until his election in May, 1890, to the United States Senate. The fame that gave him a commanding position before the country commenced with his election to the Speakership of the House of Representatives in 1883. Mr. Carlisle was recognized as one of the Democratic leaders, having won the position as the foremost debater on that side of the House. He was elected Speaker of the Forty-eighth, Forty-ninth and Fiftieth Congresses. So ably and so fairly did he discharge the duties of that important trust that he is by common consent acknowledged to be as fair a Speaker as ever wielded the gavel in the House of Representatives. This is high praise, but it is the unanimous verdict of those who sat under him during the three terms he held that high post. No appeal from a decision of his was ever sustained. His fairness was never questioned.

Mr. Carlisle has rendered great service to the country by his fight for and his elucidation of the question of revenue reform. His work on the Ways and Means Committee in the House and his speeches in the House and in the Senate in behalf of a tariff for revenue have caused him to be recognized as the chief exponent of Democratic doctrines on this subject. Mr. Carlisle has always had a strong affection for the law profession, and long before his elevation to Congress his law practice had grown to be one of the largest and most lucrative in Kentucky, but since he entered President Cleveland's Cabinet as Secretary of the Treasury, his law business has been entirely abandoned.

WILLIAM C. WHITNEY.

William Collins Whitney was born July 15, 1841, in Conway, Mass. He is a son of James S. Whitney, who was Collector of the port of Boston, and a delegate to the Democratic Convention which met at Charleston, S. C., in 1860. William C. Whitney graduated at Yale College in 1863, and at the Harvard Law School several years later. He studied law in New York City, and was admitted to the bar and practiced the profession. He was a prominent member of the Young Men's Democratic Club, which was organized in New York City in 1871, assisting very materially in its organization. He was actively engaged in the prosecution of the Tweed ring, which brought him into prominence. In 1872 he was made Inspector of the City Schools of New York, and in the same year was defeated as a candidate of the Reformed Democracy for the office of District Attorney. He took an active part in the campaign of Samuel J. Tilden for Governor of New York in 1874. He was appointed in the following year Corporation Counsel of New York City, and renominated in 1876 and 1880. He is given the credit of saving to the city, by his opposition of claims against the city, several millions of dollars. He was successful in crushing the iniquities of several corrupt rings, and was always an advocate of a reform administration. President Cleveland appointed him Secretary of the Navy in 1885. His good work in that office is shown by the creation of a fine United States navy, of which he made the nucleus by the building of several war vessels. The degree of LL. D. was conferred upon him by Yale College in 1888. His present home is at the corner of Fifth avenue and Fifty-seventh street, New York City.

DAVID B. HILL.

David Bennett Hill, of Albany, N. Y., was born at Havana, N. Y., August 29, 1843. He was educated at the public schools, graduating from the Havana Academy, at his native place, after which he clerked in a law office. In 1863 he went to Elmira, studied law, and was admitted to the bar in November, 1864, at the age of 21. He was appointed City Attorney in the same year. In 1871-72 he represented Chemung County in the State Assembly, serving on a number of important committees. He became actively engaged in politics. He was Chairman of the Democratic State Convention in 1877, and also of that of 1881. In the spring of 1882 he was elected Mayor of Elmira, and in November of the same year was chosen Lieutenant Governor of New York, on the ticket headed by Grover Cleveland, and on the resignation of Governor Cleveland in 1884, became Governor. Mr. Hill was elected Governor in 1885, re-elected in 1888, and in 1891 was elected to the United States Senate, to succeed William M. Evarts. Mr. Hill was a delegate to the National Democratic Conventions of 1876 and 1884. He has at all times discharged the duties of his various offices with credit and fidelity.

WILLIAM R. MORRISON.

Hon. William R. Morrison, a resident of Monroe County, Illinois, where he was born September 14, 1825, was educated in the common schools and at McKendree College, Lebanon, Illinois; was a private soldier in Bissell's regiment, Mexican war, and was in the battle of Buena Vista. He crossed the mountains to California in 1849, and returned to his Illinois home in 1851. Was elected Clerk of the Circuit Court of Monroe County, Illinois, 1852, resigned and was elected to the State Legislature in 1854. Was admitted to the bar in 1855. Was four times a member of the Legislature, once Speaker. Organized and commanded (for two years) the Forty-ninth Regiment, Illinois Volunteers, in the late war, and was wounded at Fort Donelson. Was eight times a member of Congress; five times a member (three times Chairman) of the Ways and Means Committee. Has been nine years a member (five times Chairman) of the Inter-State Commerce Commission. He has been active and prominent as a Democratic politician all the years of his manhood.

WILLIAM E. RUSSELL.

William E. Russell—the youngest Governor old Massachusetts ever elected—was born thirty-nine years ago from a family famous in the law profession. He is a graduate of Harvard University and of the Boston Law School. When scarcely of age he took part in the local politics of Cambridge—his home. He was soon elected an Alderman of this beautiful suburb of Boston, and at the early age of 28 was chosen Mayor of his native city. Just at that time Cambridge caught the excise fever, and its city fathers voted a prohibitory ordinance. These new regu-

lations were strictly enforced by the young Mayor, whose conduct gained him at once the respect of all, even his opponents.

At that time the old leaders of the Democratic party felt the need of the infusion of new blood if they ever expected to hold their own again in the Bay State. William

E. Russell and his great college and professional chum, John W. Corcoran, were thought worthy of sharing the counsels, struggles and political honors of the Massachusetts Democracy, and the choice proved a wise one. As a gubernatorial candidate for his party, Mr. Russell managed, in the campaigns of 1888 and 1889, to gradually reduce the old time Republican majorities. Finally, in 1890, the Russell-Corcoran ticket triumphed, and shortly after his 34th birthday, William E. Russell was inaugurated Governor, his trusted friend, Corcoran, being elected Lieutenant Governor.

In 1891, and again in 1892, the voters returned the young Governor to the executive chair, and the popularity of the brilliant tariff reformer grew apace. After his last term of office he retired to his large law practice, to which he has confined himself ever since; for this model of a reform politician is not a rich man by any means, and his earnings in his profession have to keep the pot boiling in his modest frame cottage. He married before he was 30, and is blessed with three children.

Evidently one of the leading characteristics of the man is his absolute straightforwardness. No dodging the question as far as he is concerned, and should he be chosen by the Chicago Convention, it could only be on a positive "tariff for revenue only" and "gold standard" platform.

RICHARD P. BLAND.

Richard Parks Bland was born near Hartford, Ohio County, Ky., 1835. He was left an orphan at a very early age and had to divide his time between work in the fields in the summer, and a country school, such as it was, in winter. Later he taught school himself and scraped enough money together to pay for a course of academic tuition. He finally managed to study law, and in 1855 was admitted to the bar. The next year he moved, first to California, later to Virginia City, Nevada, where he interested himself in mining ventures, while pursuing the practice of his profession. In 1860 he was elected Treasurer of Carson County, an office he retained until Nevada was admitted to the sisterhood of States. In 1865 he returned to Missouri and opened, in connection with his brother, C. C. Bland, a law office in Rolla.

In 1873 Mr. Bland was elected Congressman for Missouri as a Democrat, and was ever elected thereafter, with the exception of the present Congress (Fifty-fifth).

In 1875, being Chairman of the Committee on Mines and Mining, he introduced a bill (which became a law, with sundry and radical amendments), and which was and is yet known all over the country as the Bland bill. This law provided "that the Secretary of the Treasury shall purchase sufficient bullion to coin the minimum amount up to $2,000,000 per month in silver dollars of 412 1-2 grains, and that this dollar shall be legal tender." This law has since been repealed.

www.ingramcontent.com/pod-product-compliance
Lightning Source LLC
Chambersburg PA
CBHW020806230426
43666CB00007B/875